101 BEST
EXTRA-INCOME
OPPORTUNITIES
FOR WOMEN

101 BEST
EXTRA-INCOME
OPPORTUNITIES
FOR WOMEN

Jennifer Basye

PRIMA PUBLISHING

PRIMA PUBLISHING and colophon are registered trademarks of Prima Communications, Inc.

ISBN 1-56865-585-1

Printed in the United States of America

CONTENTS

ACKNOWLEDGMENTS

My husband, Peter Sander, and our son, Julian, kindly gave me the quiet time I needed to work on this project—thanks guys.

A special thank you to all of the women and men who took the time to answer my questions about their extra-income businesses. May you all continue to succeed and prosper.

And to everyone at Prima Publishing—from Ben and Nancy Dominitz on through each and every department—thank you all for your encouragement and enthusiasm.

INTRODUCTION

After a long week of work for a major publishing company, I get up bright and early every Saturday morning and go to the headquarters of my own company by crossing the hall into the spare bedroom. For two or three hours every week I run my own teeny-tiny, one-book publishing company, and in that time I make anywhere from $100 to $300, depending on how heavy my mail has been. I spend the time opening orders, addressing and filling envelopes with copies of my self-published budget travel book, *The Air Courier's Handbook,* answering mail from readers, sending out press packets to generate publicity, endorsing checks, and (the best part) filling out a bank deposit. Classical music fills the air as I work quietly on my own, stopping to refill my coffee cup every so often, chatting with my young son when he wanders in to show me the broken stick he found outside. I have been doing this since 1989, and I can't imagine the day when I am not actively pursuing a small business on the side, regardless of what my salaried income is. Few things are as satisfying as a dollar earned on your own, by your own talent and effort.

Bookstore shelves are filled with home-based business books of every description, each one promising that you can successfully quit your job and support yourself and your family with a business of your own. In today's tricky economy and spring-loaded job market that is a risk not all of us are able or willing to take. Better to hang on to the job that you have and use your free time to generate that much-needed second income. And if the unthinkable happens and you or your partner loses a full-time job, you will be in a much better cash position until you find another. You might also find that one day you can develop the extra-income business into a full-time pursuit with greater earnings potential than what you are paid to do for someone else. Weekends, evenings, and quiet early morning hours can be turned into a newfound cash machine of your very own as you seek out extra-income opportunities!

Within the pages of this book you will find 101 business ideas of every description that require little or no experience to achieve success—just hard work and dedication. Each chapter is filled with solid ideas to choose from, ideas that have been put into action all across the country by women just like you. Many of the business ideas here come to life with solid advice and real-life stories from women who have made it work.

With so many demands on a woman's time in today's world—everything from taking care of children to trying to keep a house and hold a full-time job—there is no sense working a second job at a fast-food joint to meet the bills or buy treats for yourself and your family when you can get started today as an extra-income entrepreneur working as much (or as little) as you want. Buying a book filled with start-up business ideas is a good first step, but it takes real courage to take the next few hesitant steps toward success. If one idea doesn't seem to work for you, instead of giving up, please try another.

Good luck, and let me hear about your success so I can include the story of you and your extra-income business in a future edition of this book!

Jennifer Basye
P.O. Box 2463
Granite Bay, CA 95746-2463

Chapter One

The Extra-Income Entrepreneur

I have been an extra-income entrepreneur ever since I was tall enough to slide a bank deposit over the marble counter to the teller. As a small child I baked cherry pie after cherry pie for my grandfather to give as gifts to his patients. Few jobs have paid as well since. I created sequin jewelry as an enterprising teen, and started a small campus news bulletin while in college. Since graduating I have spent the work week happily employed in the book business, but I have never given up the thrill, the freedom, and the big financial rewards of working for myself in my spare time.

What kind of woman needs an extra-income opportunity, you ask? Any hardworking and dedicated woman who works as a salaried or hourly wage employee for someone else, but would enjoy the benefits of creating more money in her spare time by working for herself: mothers who have chosen to stay home with small children, energetic teenage girls looking for ways to earn a little spending money or start a savings account, college students who need a way to stretch their tuition loans, and retired women who just aren't ready to stay away from the business world for good. Perhaps you are an office worker in the employ of a major corporation. Sure, you like your job but you would also enjoy a larger paycheck. This year's prospects for a raise look bleak for everyone, but what will you tell your son when he asks about summer camp? How can you tell your daughter that the budget is too tight for ballet lessons? And what if one of the kids needs braces? How can you meet your New Year's resolution to pay your credit cards off faster and end this year debt free?

What you need is what my husband Peter calls a SAM—a Source of Additional Money! Start working for yourself as an extra-income entrepreneur, a spare time or "weekend entrepreneur" with a creative SAM, and reward yourself with a more secure financial future.

Even women who make a top salary enjoy the freedom and excitement of having an extra-income business. Perhaps you don't have to worry about meeting your basic bills, but wouldn't it be nice to have extra money for a trip to Hawaii this year instead of a long weekend in your own state?

Anyone can earn extra income. All across the country women just like you—sales clerks, teachers, lawyers, stay-at-home moms, real estate agents, librarians, students, and others from all walks of life—are choosing to add to their bank accounts by working part time for themselves. You work hard all week long in your regular job—why add to the stress by taking a second job working for another company? Take your time and your financial destiny into your own hands and work as much or as little as you like. After all, you're the boss! Another plus to being an extra-income entrepreneur is that with most of these business ideas you can stop and start according to your cash needs. Chances are, though, that when that extra money starts coming in you won't want to stop!

Not every type of business is suited to the needs of an extra-income entrepreneur. The business ideas outlined here are specially chosen to suit part-time work, with a minimum of investment, experience, and overhead. For most of these businesses you will not need an office, just a spare corner of your house or apartment. I trust you, the reader, to investigate your local business laws and regulations and make certain that you follow them closely. This is important, as extra-income entrepreneurs owe it to each other to follow the letter of the law in order not to give the profession a bad name. I also trust you to report your extra income in your annual tax return. Please consult a tax planner if you are not certain how to do this. Honest people sleep easier at night. Remember to be good to your customers and deliver 110% of what you have promised. Happy customers are always your best (and least expensive!) advertisement.

While investigating extra-income opportunities around the country, I have stumbled across an interesting development in our society that I believe holds the key to success for any woman who is looking for ways to generate more money. Our lifestyles are changing rapidly and four distinct types of people seem to be emerging:

1. Due to the stagnant business economy, there are large numbers of employed people whose incomes have leveled off while their bills have grown. These people have a real need for a SAM—a Source of Additional Money!

2. And then there are the relatively successful folks who enjoy a SAM to help them do a few extra things in life, like buy fancy camping equipment or enjoy weekly dinners at a favorite restaurant.

3. There is a group of working people who are so caught up in their careers that they have little or no time to take care of the basic things in life like cooking, cleaning, and running errands. What little free time they do have is spent relaxing, traveling, or pursuing hobbies. These folks just don't want to deal with the mess that projects around the house can create—they want to skip the sweat and frustration of certain types of jobs.

4. An ever-increasing segment of the American population is "silvering," a popular advertising term for growing old. As we age, we are less and less able to do the simple things in life that we have taken for granted all these years—drive a car to the grocery store, keep our windows shiny and clean, or weed the vegetable garden.

The financial needs of the first two groups—the group whose incomes have leveled off, and the group who wants a few more of life's extras—can be met by designing businesses and services that cater to the needs of the other two groups. And the wonderful secret is that as the years pass, their needs will not diminish, but only increase! Here is a perfect built-in market for extra-income entrepreneurs.

Among the business ideas that follow you will find some that are simple, old-fashioned, uncomplicated businesses and services that were common years ago but seem to have disappeared. This is another key to success for women looking for extra-income opportunities: Look to the past for ideas that have fallen to the wayside in today's complicated world. It is perhaps too late to revive the role of the colorful countryside tinker traveling from town to town to fix cooking pots, but there are many other great ideas out there.

A successful businessperson is always on the lookout for new ideas and ways to take advantage of trends. Always watch for what's hot and find a way to make money from it. Buzzwords nowadays are "green" (environmentally sensitive) and "simple living." Who knows what will emerge as the next trend in coming years? I have included a few ideas that fit in with current trends, but there are doubtless many more out there to be developed. Several years ago two brothers in Oregon spotted a growing trend—gourmet coffees—and fashioned a part-time business running a small espresso stand in the corner of a grocery store parking lot. Yes, it is an adult version of a lemonade stand, but it sure does attract the customers! Look for their success story in Chapter 7, "Cooking Up Dollars," and look for a related idea to help you capitalize on the growing gourmet coffee trend under the heading of *Home Coffee Delivery*. Keep your eyes, ears, and even taste buds open to spot trends and capitalize on them as they are emerging. Pay close attention to the stories in magazines, newspapers, and on television—you never know when the right idea will present itself.

To help you find a weekend business that suits you, the next chapters are filled with business ideas grouped in several different ways. These chapters include:

Back to Basics—Elbow Grease and a Strong Back

Among the businesses best suited to extra-income entrepreneurs are those requiring a strong back, a steady hand with a hammer, and a willingness to get your hands dirty. Throughout history man (and woman) has relied on labor to produce financial rewards, and it is just as true today. Fortunately, wages have risen since the days of feudalism! Handiwork, repairs, and odd jobs are businesses that are quick to start and pay cash, and customers can frequently be found in your own neighborhood. This chapter details businesses for women with a knack for fixing things, or a willingness to do a bit of dirty work or physical labor.

Old-Fashioned Money—Look to the Past for Your Financial Future

There are many plain-old, tried-and-true ways to make extra money in your spare time, and they can still work for you! Garage and yard sales, small farming projects like herb gardens and cut flowers, and the centuries-old tradition of beekeeping are just a few, but in this chapter you will also find many other inventive ways in which women can use tested money-making methods to their advantage. The chapter also includes business ideas for services that used to exist (such as basic delivery services), that are needed more than ever in this fast-paced world.

Crafty Business—Money-Making Ideas for Craft Fairs

Always doing something with your hands? Turn your hobby into a money machine with these ideas for profitable craft projects. Learn how to turn hand-rolled beeswax candles into cash, make and market wooden planter boxes, fashion trendy chili wreaths for year-round sales, and paint dried gourds. Selling handmade items at craft fairs and bazaars can not only provide steady extra income, but a great deal of fun for the whole family to boot!

Odds and Ends—Great SAMs That Defy Categories

These ideas just don't fit anywhere else! Perhaps your skills and interests also defy categories, and if so this is the chapter for you. Here are many ways to make extra money that range from the wild to the weird (leading tours of graveyards?), but all are wonderfully fun moneymakers.

Available Talent—Opportunities for Artists, Musicians, and Writers

For those women lucky enough to be gifted with artistic or musical talent, many opportunities are available. Face painting for children is a great way to use artistic skills; custom-made stationery is another. These businesses are carefully explained in this chapter, along with many other ways for talented folks to earn extra cash.

Cooking Up Dollars— Making Money in the Kitchen

Come the weekends, we all like to indulge a bit . . . what better way to make extra money than to cater to that universal craving for tasty food? Specialty food vendors, bakeries, and gourmet fruit stands are solid ways for entrepreneurs to cash in on a need; so are specialized services, such as custom cooking for professional people. Food trends emerge quickly, you can cash in on many of them.

Long Shots—Great Ideas for Special People

Here are quirky ideas that won't work for just anyone, but maybe they will work for you! These ideas require special talents (like writing and publishing), special locations (tourist areas), or special interests (antique clothing). Real cash bonanzas are out there if you have all of the special ingredients to make it work!

Moms at Home—Extra Money for Entrepreneurial Mothers

Many of the ideas covered in earlier chapters throughout the book are perfect for mothers at home with small children. This chapter details the top ten ways for stay-at-home moms to earn extra income from home, and directs you to other great businesses that will suit this situation.

At the end of each chapter there is a section called *Thinking It Through* in which I give a roundup of special considerations that the businesses described in the chapter might require. Brass-tacks elements like insurance, licensing, marketing, and other hard facts are discussed. Read this section for important information before you make decisions regarding which SAM will suit your needs, skills, and interests.

Each potential business is carefully explained in a simple fashion to help you decide if it is right for you. Special requirements are explained and drawbacks revealed. In many cases I have included interviews with real-life entrepreneurs who have successfully used these ideas to add to their income. These men and women give no-nonsense advice about what it takes to make it work, and how much money you can expect to earn.

These successful extra-income entrepreneurs also give lots of advice on marketing, finding customers, and getting paid. Start reading now and find the perfect SAM (Source of Additional Money) for you! Take a close look at the various chapters, flip to the section that seems right for your background, and find out how to join the growing ranks of the extra-income entrepreneurs.

Chapter Two

Back to Basics—
Elbow Grease and
a Strong Back

Some of the best-paying and easiest-to-establish methods for building extra income involve good, honest, hard, physical work. Remember that group of people whom we identified in Chapter 1 who don't want to get dirty doing the basic things in life anymore? What about the growing population of aging folks who are less able to do things for themselves? These are definitely the target groups for clients and customers for many of the business ideas in this chapter. So roll up your sleeves and get to work!

Car Detailer

Sunny Saturday afternoons used to be the traditional time for Dad and the kids to go out to the driveway with a sloshing bucket of soapy water, a ragged towel rescued from the rag bin, armed with a coiled green hose, ready to give the family car its weekly washing. Well, times have changed. Dad is at the office on Saturday and the kids are playing Nintendo. Though we all may long for the way life used to be, we should also rejoice that yet another opportunity has been created for women entrepreneurs!

Becoming a personal car detailer fills a real need in the marketplace, for a number of reasons:

1. Many working people have less time nowadays to wash their cars themselves. They would much rather be out on the golf course or taking in a Saturday matinee.

2. With the uncertain economy, people are keeping their cars longer and postponing the purchase of a shiny new car. The car that they have been driving for years could use a good detailing to give it a new car look and help maintain its value.

3. People who own fancy cars love to lavish care and attention on them, but don't necessarily want to do it themselves.

4. Automatic car washes—although convenient and popular—just don't do the thorough job that a hand detailer can offer. It's like comparing a weekly quick-clean to a thorough spring cleaning!

5. Having a car detailed is a great way to improve its looks just before the owner puts it up for sale. That extra bit of shine helps keep the price up.

I learned what a great income generator car detailing could be from my friend Margaret Cable. As a full-time student, she supplemented her student loans by establishing several steady clients whose cars she would detail every other week. For a thorough car detailing, her rate was $50. I talked to Margaret about what was involved in becoming a successful car detailer. Her advice was encouraging: "I made great extra money for years as a car detailer. After a few jobs I had a reputation as a super perfectionist, and that helped me get other clients. Starting the business was easy. I went to a high-end auto supply store and invested in their best car wash, car care, and wax products. Customers like to see you using top brands on their cars; it sure helps them write out that check for $50 at the end! Always use good chamois cloths on their cars, that looks impressive too." Margaret's best customers were real estate agents—agents frequently drive clients around in their cars and need to impress them with their shiny clean auto.

To get started as a car detailer, here are the supplies you will need: several spray bottles, window cleaner, towels for windows, a squeegee, a toothbrush for detail work, tire black, instant brake dust remover spray, several good heavy-duty sponges, scrub brush with a long handle, spray hose attachment, portable vacuum cleaner, leather care products like mink oil, several chamois cloths, Ivory soap, furniture polish for wood and plastic interiors, wax, rubbing compound, and a big box of Q-tips for the really fine detail work. You will have many of these things lying around your house, but I will repeat the advice that the fancier the products you use and the better-looking your basic equipment, the higher the price the customer will be willing to pay. Think "image."

Setting Rates

Personal car detailing service at the client's home or office should begin at $40, higher for trucks and vans. As you gain a reputation, or are lucky enough to be in an expensive urban area, your rates may be somewhat higher. It is possible, but of course not required, that some of your customers may add a tip to the price when they pay you. And remember, this is a long way from the days when a kid would wash your car for a dollar. Act like a professional, do a good job, and you will succeed.

Finding Clients

Take a tip from Margaret Cable, try real estate agents first! Make up flyers and business cards advertising your personal car detailing service and drop them off at real estate offices. Be sure to chat up the receptionist or office manager; perhaps you should even offer to do their car for free, to get the word around about your services. Live near a medical office complex? Put your flyers under the window of all those doctors' cars out there in the parking lot! Drop leaflets off at the doorstep in ritzy neighborhoods. Satisfied customers are your best advertisement, and standing in someone's driveway doing a great job in full view of the neighborhood is like a free billboard and will help pull in the customers. Always behave as though someone were watching you (they probably are), don't play loud music, and don't let your friends hang around and talk to you while you are working. Work quietly and quickly; your customers will appreciate it.

Margaret Cable's Recommended
Steps for Terrific Car Detailing

1. Wipe off all windows with a clean, dry cloth. Wash the interior windows and vacuum the interior.
2. Spray brake dust remover on wheels.
3. Use the long-handled brush on the wheels, then rinse the wheels with a hose.
4. Wash the entire vehicle with mild soap like Ivory (but remember, the better the brand, the higher the price you can charge!), using sponges to clean the surface and a toothbrush to really clean the grill and the chrome pieces, then rinse the entire car.
5. Rub the entire car dry with a chamois cloth, wringing the chamois dry when necessary. Finish the drying process with ordinary terry cloth towels.
6. Wax the entire car (if a client requests that you use rubbing compound first, charge an extra $15). Modern silicon polishes are as effective as traditional wax, are easier to use, and have solvents to remove bugs. Use a good brand.
7. Wipe the entire interior with a damp cloth and use vinyl spray or leather treatment spray where appropriate. Lemon furniture polish is a good touch here. Empty ashtrays of trash and butts and wipe them clean.
8. Do the exterior windows, using the squeegee to avoid streaks.
9. Apply chrome polish to the wheels to give them a brand-new look.
10. Apply tire black (carefully!) to all tires using a disposable sponge.
11. Wipe down exterior black plastic and rubber parts with furniture polish or mink oil. If you use mink oil, wipe down with a dry cloth afterwards (otherwise dust will stick to the excess material).
12. Finished! Collect your pay and go on to the next car!

Personal car detailing is a terrific SAM that you can start and succeed at with little or no money. It is also possible to go the high-end route by purchasing a franchise from a national company. Check the ads in many of the small business magazines and you will find the names of companies that offer franchises.

On-Site Car Detailing

Here is a great variation on making extra income as a car detailer. A father and son in Roseville, California, have begun offering their services as mobile car detailers to folks while they work out at the gym. By leafleting the cars in the gym's parking lot (with the manager's permission, of course) and garnering mentions in the club newsletter, they have been able to build up a steady clientele of folks who are happy to have someone buff and polish their cars while they buff and polish their bodies! What businesses can you think of that attract folks who leave their cars sitting in the parking lot for several hours? Approach those businesses about offering on-site car detailing to their clients. The actual process of detailing the car will be exactly like that described earlier, with the exception of the fact that you will have to invest in a mobile water tank and sprayer. You won't be able to rely on using the hose in the parking lot.

Bathroom/Tile Detailer

Sure, you've heard of having your car detailed, but having your bathroom detailed? Now that is strange. Well, not as strange as you think. There are in fact housecleaners who specialize in doing nothing but cleaning bathrooms until every last surface, nook, and cranny gleams. And there are also folks who specialize in cleaning and revitalizing tile showers, floors, and other tile surfaces. After awhile tile and grout tends to look a bit scruffy and could use a good cleaning.

How do you go about starting a side business detailing bathrooms or cleaning tile? Start first in your own bathroom and on your own tile surfaces, testing which of the commercial cleaning products works best. Many of the tools used in detailing cars (see the description just before this one) the same for detailing bathrooms. Toothbrushes or other small hard brushes will be used in exactly the same way to reach into small spaces and achieve the "I can't believe you cleaned there!" effect that will please your customers.

Christmas Light Installer

Once a year an opportunity to make excellent extra money appears. Installing and removing decorative outdoor Christmas lights is a great idea for folks who like the holiday look, but don't have the time to do it themselves, are too old to manage, or are afraid of heights.

Most moms have had experience untangling the lights every year, checking to make sure no bulbs are burnt out, and spending an afternoon on a ladder hanging up the annual light show. Full-time computer technology student Michelle Barnes, 19, started Michelle's Christmas Lights Services after several years of installing Christmas lights for family and friends. She decided that charging for the service would be an excellent way to earn extra money for college fees and books.

Unlike costly decorating firms which provide the lights themselves as well as installation, Michelle advises part-time entrepreneurs to work with their customer's own Christmas lights: "With the economy and everything, I think a lot of people just want to work with what they already have." Michelle charges $25 for installation on a one-story house, and then returns several weeks later to remove them for an additional $20. A two-story house would run the owner about $50 for Michelle's services. Extension cords are included in the price, but if clip fasteners are required she charges an extra $6. The tools required to run a seasonal business like this are minimal: a ladder, staple gun, clips, and hooks. How much easier can it get? A similar custom lighting business was recently featured in *Money* magazine as one of just four of "America's best home businesses." The fellow featured in the article had built his business up to the point where he made more than $100,000 a year!

Start looking for customers in mid-November, perhaps even leafleting cars in grocery store parking lots while folks are doing their Thanksgiving Day shopping (check with the store's owner first). Picking out a fancy neighborhood in which to leaflet is also important, since many of these homeowners might feel a real sense of competition with their neighbors when it comes to decorating for the holidays, and they will be relieved to have professional help at one-upping the Joneses.

In addition to installing and removing lights, another handy service could be offered to your clients at the same time. For an extra $15 you could offer to come back after Christmas and haul away the Christmas tree and take it to a mulcher, thereby helping both the customer and the environment!

Cleaning Recreational Vehicles

RVs are everywhere! Retired couples vacation for weeks on end in their recreational vehicles, returning home happy but exhausted and only too pleased to pay a skilled person to give the RV a good post-trip cleaning. Specialize in cleaning only the interiors and build your reputation on that. Finding customers for this business is simple, just look up and down the street! RVs parked on the street and in driveways are simple targets for leaflets; either drop one on the front porch of the house or tuck it under the windshield wiper of the RV itself. Another great way to find clients for this specialized cleaning service is to head down to the local RV sales store. Once RVers have purchased their travel-home-on-wheels, they return again and again to the dealer to buy after-market gadgets for their RV. Posting flyers or business cards at the dealer is a terrific way to pick up business. Many dealerships have waiting room areas with bulletin boards sporting information about RV owners' clubs, groups, and get-togethers. This would be an ideal spot to post information about your RV cleaning service. Contact the members of those clubs with flyers, a useful way to advertise your service.

A thorough cleaning job in a medium-size recreational vehicle will take approximately three hours. As you become more skilled and develop a routine you may be able to do a fine job in much less time. The price for a post-trip cleaning should be between $50 and $75. Large RVs and exceptionally dirty RVs should run closer to $80 for an interior cleaning. Washing the exterior of an RV is quite another matter and the price should be negotiated separately.

To clean the interior of an RV you will need the following supplies and equipment: a canister-style vacuum cleaner with crevice tool attachments, dust rags and cloths, bathroom cleaner, floor cleaning products, mop, sink scouring products, oven cleaner, vinyl cleaner, window cleaner, empty garbage bags, and a good sponge.

The preferred method of cleaning an RV after weeks on the road is as follows:

1. Always start with the dirtiest tasks—clean the freezer and refrigerator, stove and oven, and the entire kitchen area. Remove all items from kitchen drawers and cupboards and vacuum inside thoroughly before replacing.

2. Starting from the back of the RV and working your way to the front, begin cleaning all surface areas like table tops, counter tops, the tops of shelves, seat covers, windowsills, and dashboards. Vacuum when necessary then use a good vinyl cleaner and furniture polish on the appropriate surfaces. Check to see if the ashtrays have been used and empty and clean them if necessary.

3. Clean the entire bathroom thoroughly. This area really takes a beating during a long trip and the owners will appreciate a good job in this room.

4. Clean the entire sleeping area. Vacuum carefully around the edges of the bed using crevice tools; lots of dirt and sand end up here! Clean the closet area.

5. Clean all windows and mini-blinds.

6. Moving from back to front again, do all of the floors, first with the vacuum, then mop and wax.

7. Collect your pay from the satisfied owners, ask for recommendations of any other RVers who might need your services, and head to

the next job! And remember, smile every time you see an RV out on the road. The owners will surely be needing your help soon.

Detailing Recreational Vehicles

In addition to cleaning the insides of RVs, it is possible to specialize in detailing the outsides. I spoke to one entrepreneur who had been detailing RVs for several years: "You do have to specialize in RV detailing; because of the aluminum and so forth it is quite a bit different from detailing cars. It costs a lot of money to have an RV repainted, so what I do is 're-condition' it instead. A paint job for a motor home is going to run around $5,000, but I can totally recondition it for anywhere from $600 to $1,200." This fellow was very pleased with the extra income but was not at all willing to give me any details about his business. I guess it is so hot that he doesn't want anyone else doing it! So if detailing and reconditioning RVs sounds interesting to you, I'm afraid that you will have to go out and learn it all on your own.

Cobweb Cleaning and Removal Service

It's happened to everybody once or twice. You finally get up the nerve to invite a few new friends over to dinner, and after everyone has settled in to enjoy the evening you spy a cobweb hanging right over the sideboard on which your beautiful buffet dinner has been set. Those pesky cobwebs are annoying, but they also present a SAM that can snare some extra cash for you! Why not run a part-time cobweb cleaning and removal service to make the world safe for casual entertaining? By offering your clients a biweekly or monthly cobweb service you will be tending to an unpleasant task that most people would happily prefer to hire out.

Cobwebs occur both indoors and out. You can either specialize in one area or take care of the whole property indoors and out for a larger fee. Style your cobweb service after the monthly pest-spraying services, always arrive on the same pre-arranged day of the week or month, do the job, and leave behind a small payment envelope for your customer to mail back to you.

There is very little danger involved in removing cobwebs; the most dangerous element is that you may have to reach up into cathedral ceilings or outdoor eaves to track down those pesky spiders and their webs. In North America, the only spider that poses a serious threat is the "black widow," which may be found in or near woodpiles close to the ground, often in a garage or similar area. Chances are that you will never see one of these small black-and-orange marked spiders, but do be careful. Guard your personal safety with caution and the proper equipment.

You will need the following tools for a cobweb removal service: a cobweb removing tool, an extension pole, broom, bucket, and paper bags for your "catch." Many home improvement, hardware, or even grocery stores sell a product called a Webster, which has a big soft circular brush about eight inches in diameter attached to a short extension handle. This handle can reach 8 to 10 feet off the ground, but you can add firepower to your tool by adding an extension pole to extend your effectiveness to 12 to 16 feet. Spiders and their webs can be pretty high off the ground!

Removing the cobwebs themselves is a straightforward process. First find them by looking *everywhere*! Ceiling corners, edges, window corners, and behind furniture are popular indoor spider homes. For outdoor spiders and their webs, look in eaves, window frames, door frames (every door frame in America has at least one spider web on it somewhere!), and light fixtures. You will soon develop a sixth sense about where to find webs, and you will learn the popular spots in your clients' houses. Spiders are brainless enough that they build webs over and over in the same spot.

Once you find a cobweb, you can't just shove the remover into it and scrub it free from the surface or you will end up with a bigger problem than before. Remember, cobwebs are sticky and dirt and dust cling to them; if you smear it into a wall you will now have to clean a sticky balled-up cobweb off a wall. Instead, approach the cobweb delicately, as sportscasters like to say, with "touch." Use the remover to make contact with the cobweb, then slowly twist the remover while being careful to stay away from adjacent surfaces. The cobweb itself will stick to the remover; once detached you can slowly bring it away from the wall. Every so often you will have to clean the wound-up webs off your remover; this is what the paper bags are for! And what about the spider? Many times the spider will come down along with the web. Dispose of it in a reasonable way—smashing is not recommended! To reduce your future workload you can use the pesticide solution. Discuss this in advance with your customer; not everyone feels the same about the use of insecticides. If you do use a bug killer use it sparingly, it is very strong and will leave an unpleasant odor.

When setting rates for your cobweb removal service take into account the size of the house and frequency of the visits. Charge more for the first visit then a smaller fee for recurring visits. Basic indoor service on a standard-size house should be a monthly rate of $20. Two-story houses, cathedral ceilings, or other quirks add to the cost. Also consider the amount of time that the project will take you, and be certain that your rates guarantee that you make at least $20 an hour for your time.

Dog Doo Removal Service

Yes, this service does exactly what you think it does. What some people think is just a yucky and annoying job can mean scooping up dollars for you. Overlook the obvious jokes that your friends will make when they hear about your new venture SAM and concentrate on making money. As our lives become more complicated, many of us turn to man's best friend for solace and comfort. After a tough day at the office, what could be better than curling up on the couch in front of the VCR with a dog sleeping on your lap? Unfortunately, although we enjoy having our pets around, we just don't seem to have the time to go out into the yard and pick up the . . . well, you know. And this is where you come in! Working with your clients to design a convenient route you can easily establish a Saturday or Sunday morning routine, dropping in just once a week to clear the yard of droppings. Average fees for this service can range from $6 to $10 per dog per week. Just think, if you have only ten steady clients with twelve dogs "producing" for you regularly, that adds as much as $480 to your bank account each month for just a few hours work. Call this idea a SUPER SAM!

I talked to Rhonda Jurkowski at Waggin' Tails about how she got started in the dog dropping removal business. "When I moved to California from Canada I had a few different ideas for businesses that I wanted to try, and this one seemed to have the biggest potential audience. At first I thought that my biggest group of clients would be handicapped people, but it turns out that by far the most typical client for Waggin' Tails is a double-income couple with kids. I guess they want the typical American family look with a couple of kids and a nice dog, but when it comes time to pick up after the dog they just don't have time."

Rhonda charges $6 for the first dog, and $3 for every additional dog per client. Most clients have her come by once a week, but some like the yard cleaned two, three, and even five times a week! Six dollars five times a week—that's $30 from one customer alone! A business picking up dog droppings is perfect for a weekend entrepreneur, as most folks want their yard cleaned on the weekends.

Not very many supplies are needed in this business, just a steady supply of medium-size garbage bags, gloves, a shovel, and a rake. How much simpler can life be?

After two and a half years in business, Rhonda Jurkowski has her equipment down to a science—she uses a big lobby pan (the thing that you see employees at McDonald's using to sweep and pick up trash at the same time) and a three-pronged garden tool that she has lengthened by adding a 3-foot piece of PVC pipe. "Line the lobby pan with a garbage bag before you pick up a yard, and dispose of the droppings in the customer's own outdoor garbage can. If you take it away with you to dispose of somewhere else, you will need a permit for hauling hazardous waste!"

The best way to find customers is to post notices in the window at your local pet stores and grocery stores. Ask the owner or manager for permission, of course. Letting veterinarians and dog trainers know about your service will be a boost. The local animal shelter is also a great place to advertise. Perhaps you could offer a one-week service free for a newly adopted dog; once the new owner gets used to your service it could become a steady account. If there is no one else in your area offering the same service, the chances that you can get media coverage are very good. Call the newspaper and ask to speak to the business editor. He or she may be quite intrigued by your enterprising business and may very well write an article about it. Another good bet for free media attention is morning radio disk jockeys. This is exactly the kind of thing that they would love to make jokes about on the air. Send a press release to their attention, giving details about your service, and be sure to include your phone number. They will, of course, make many silly jokes on the radio about you, but shrug it off and enjoy the free publicity.

Dog Exercise and Play Groups

Here is another extra-income opportunity that an animal lover can easily develop. We all know how much Americans love their dogs; sometimes it seems that every household has one or two. But with the fast-paced lives that keep so many of us away from home for nine or ten hours a day, are Fido and Fluffy getting all of the attention, interaction, and exercise they need? Enter the clever entrepreneur who develops a business to take advantage of this situation!

Yes, there really are doggie play groups already in existence. Lesley Sager Levine runs Pet-Estrian Services in Belmont, Massachusetts, and offers 45-minute play sessions for dogs, in her own backyard. An enterprising Malibu, California, woman runs the dogs of the rich and famous up and down that beautiful beach to keep them (and herself at the same time) in tip-top shape.

Setting Rates

Try to price your services in such a way that your clients can afford to have you exercise their pets on a weekly basis. A reasonable weekly fee would be $10 per dog per hour.

Finding Clients

Advertising your services as a doggie exerciser could be done in the same way as the previous business of dog doo removal. Your best bets would be to post flyers and business cards at pet stores and veterinarians' offices. And, like the doo removal service, this idea is wacky enough to attract some free publicity if you put together a press release to send to your local media.

Graffiti Removal Service

Graffiti on public and private buildings is an unfortunate fact of life nowadays, but the hardworking spare-time entrepreneur can take advantage of this trend by cleaning up after graffiti artists! "You'll never have enough police to patrol graffiti," says Steve Lindner of Graffiti Control Services. "Most graffiti vandals want their mess to be seen. If you get rid of it, they might come back. But after a second time, they'll move on to another building."

Sound like hard work? Yes, but what mother doesn't already perform "graffiti removal" in some fashion or another in her own home anyway? Go out into the community and be paid for it instead.

Depending on the size of the job, Lindner's fees range from $50 for a very small job to a whopping $10,000 for a full-scale graffiti-proofing treatment for a large building. To remove graffiti he uses several techniques, depending on the surface of the building:

1. On smooth-surface buildings, graffiti can sometimes be scrubbed off using basic cleaning solvents.
2. Brick surfaces need to be sandblasted with fine sand to remove the paint or ink.
3. Serious graffiti must be painted over. Match the original color by consulting with a local paint company for the best results.

Chicago tuckpointer Dan Webb donates his services on the weekends to help keep his neighborhood graffiti-free, and he suggests that working for free would be an ideal way to develop the skills needed to start a part-time business in this field.

Once you are confident in your skills, you are ready to begin charging for your service. Merchants' associations and business associations like the Chamber of Commerce can be an excellent steady source of clients for a graffiti remover. Find out when local organizations meet and attend meetings to meet members. Or hop in your car and cruise the streets until you spot a graffiti-covered business: There are potential customers on every corner.

Steve Lindner has taken his part-time service one step further and developed a special coating for buildings that allows graffiti to be wiped off. He hopes to sell the mixture in large quantities to city maintenance departments across the country. But until Steve's coating protects every building in the land there will be plenty of opportunities for you to "clean up"!

Janitorial Services

"A janitorial business is a perfect small business for women looking to earn extra income," George Bingham advises. "It is very easy to enter the market, and just as easy to get out when you no longer need the extra money. And the start-up costs are extremely low. To do most janitorial work in offices all you really need is a bucket, a mop, a vacuum cleaner, and some miscellaneous cleaning supplies. What could be easier?"

George and his wife Beanie started a small janitorial service as an additional source of income when his regular business ran out of steam. "Get yourself a business card and walk out there and start knocking on doors in office buildings. Once you have signed up one client you can use that client as a reference to attract others."

Running a small janitorial service at night and on the weekends is a perfect way for a whole family to work together to make money. George says that it is becoming more and more common to see a husband, wife, and teenagers all cleaning together on the job. The work goes faster and everyone can contribute to the family business.

Rates are very competitive in the janitorial business. Check to see what the average is in your part of the country before setting your prices. In the Western states the standard rate is 5.5 cents per foot. Always insist on measuring the area yourself, George suggests.

"In real estate everyone exaggerates the square footage when they try to sell an office building, but when hiring a janitorial service they always underestimate to try to shave costs! Be careful." The basic rate only covers vacuuming, dusting, and cleaning bathroom areas. More profitable aspects of the business are "tags," or extras like carpet cleaning or window washing. These jobs are not done as a regular part of your nightly or weekly janitorial service, but rather once or twice a year for an agreed-upon price.

Since the rates among janitorial services are so competitive, the best way to gain an edge on your competition is through superior service. Always be on time, do a thorough job, and leave the office looking undisturbed. This last piece of advice is crucial, as whenever anything is missing or broken in an office a finger will immediately be pointed at the janitorial service. Protect yourself by carrying insurance.

As with a housecleaning business, there are emerging opportunities in the janitorial business for "green" cleaning methods that are easy on the planet. If there is not another environmentally correct janitorial service operating in your area, this may be the way to distinguish yourself from the competition right away. Read the *Holistic Housecleaning* section in Chapter 6 to gain a better understanding of this issue. The ability to clean fast and well is important when you are trying to clean more than one office building a night. Best-selling author and cleaning entrepreneur Don Aslett has made cleaning a science, and many hints for fast methods may be found in his books:

Cleaning Up for a Living
Don Aslett
Betterway Publications
$12.95

Do I Dust or Vacuum First?
Don Aslett
Writer's Digest Books
$9.95

Organic Lawn Service

In Chapter 1, I talked about the need for a successful extra-income entrepreneur to pay attention and spot trends and needs as they occur. More and more Americans are worrying about the effect that chemicals have on the environment, and businesses that cater to this situation are truly on the cutting edge. You don't get much more "cutting edge" than Christl Saed and her organic lawn service!

After ten years in a dental office Christl decided to go back to school full time and needed a part-time business to support her schooling. By combining her love of nature and the outdoors with her devotion to organic garden care, she has created a very successful business. "I'm not a 'mow-and-blow' operation, that is what my clients appreciate most," she said, as she described her business to me over coffee. "I use a hand-mower to cut grass and a good old-fashioned rake to clean up the leaves. There are lots of people out there who are absolutely passionate in their hatred of gas-powered leaf blowers and the noise that they make. Exhaust, dust, and leaves blowing everywhere—it is awful for the environment!" By offering organic lawn care instead of the usual fare, Christl has found a profitable

niche in an established market. After just six months in the business, working just twenty hours a week, she is able to support
herself while attending college. In addition to cutting lawns and
cleaning up leaves, she also offers pruning and light trimming,
weeding, and removing annuals, and she frequently makes suggestions to her clients about which plants might work best for
them. Two other services that she hopes to add once she gains
expertise are a composting and compost management service,
and organic pest management. By expanding her range of services beyond cutting and raking she is able to make money
throughout the winter season when grass grows slowly. Since
by its very nature this is a "low-tech" business, start-up costs are
low. In addition to a hand-mower and several sturdy rakes,
Christl has the following:

knee pads	pruning shears
spades and shovels	loppers
big plastic bags to move grass	hedge shears
and clippings (but don't bag	
things permanently as it is	
terrible for the environment!)	

Rates are either hourly or a flat fee for regular customers.
Depending on your area, you should be able to charge a minimum of $8 an hour for your service, and Christl suggests
charging $10 an hour for one-time-only jobs. Advertising in
publications that appeal to the organically minded homeowner
are your best bet for finding clients. Try small community
newspapers or natural food co-op newsletters. Most food co-
ops also have community bulletin boards where you can post
information about your service.

"I love the fact that what I do is a part of the solution to the
earth's problems," says Christl, "And I'm making more people
aware of the environment at the same time. I set my own hours,
work in the open air, and get paid to learn more about plants,
soil, and moisture. As more and more people become aware of
the connection between their lifestyle and the state of the earth,
the opportunities for this kind of a service will increase dramatically."

Window Washer

When Sarah Brooks and two college friends couldn't find part-time summer jobs in Sacramento, they formed their own window-washing collective. "It was cheap to start up. I think that's why we chose window washing. We got started for around $30," Sarah told me on the phone, taking a few minutes off from studying for finals in agri-business to tell me the details of having a window-washing business.

"We bought a couple of supplies like squeegees, several spray water bottles, and a cobweb remover. We borrowed a retractable ladder, and mixed up our own secret window-washing formula. After testing the formula on our parents' windows to make sure that it worked, we started to look for clients.

"Going door to door is not an effective method of finding customers; it takes too much of your time. Posting flyers at local grocery stores in our neighborhood was pretty effective, and an even more effective method was giving our flyers to local housecleaners to pass out to their clients. We got a lot of customers that way. Once we started working and the word got out that we did a good job; we got lots of referrals. An extra $100 dollars a week? Sure, we made that much and more!"

Sarah has quite a bit of advice for other women interested in starting up a part-time window-washing business: "The most difficult part in the beginning is deciding your price. It takes a fair amount of skill to appraise a job; each house is different and the windows require different treatment. Those little paned windows are tough and take forever! Takes twice as long to wash that kind as the big picture windows. Two-story houses and houses with high ceilings are more, too. Our basic rate for an ordinary ranch-style house was $60. It would take between 3 and 4 hours to complete a house like that, inside and out. If we just did the outside, we would charge less. Spend some time checking out your competitors' prices. Our prices were comparable, and we promised our clients 'no streaks.' That was a tough promise to keep sometimes, but we did!"

An interesting marketing technique that Sarah and her partners used was a follow-up thank you note. Each and every one of their clients received a thank-you note in the mail a few days after the job was completed. Not only did this serve to reinforce the good work that had been done, it encouraged their clients to recommend the window washers to their friends. And many did just that: The partners were busy all summer long. Their business was so successful that they plan to revive it next summer!

A part-time window-washing business works best during the spring and summer months. With the bright light streaming in, homeowners are keenly aware of how dirty their windows have become and start to think of having them washed. The daylight hours are longer and part-timers can fit weekday window-washing jobs in. Saturdays and Sundays are ideal, of course, and it is possible to fit three or four jobs in during the weekend.

Alerting local real estate agents to your window-washing service is also a good move. As houses go on the market in the spring and summer months, shiny clean windows help increase a house's curb appeal.

On-Site Neck Massage

Tension is everywhere, and what better way to work out the tension than a neck and shoulder massage? What used to seem like a luxury is fast becoming an ordinary thing, thanks to the arrival of businesses like The Great American Backrub in New York City, where you can pop in off the street for a 15-minute massage. "Drop-in" foot massage kiosks are starting to appear in malls around the country to pamper the feet of tired shoppers and give them the energy to tackle just one more store-wide sale. . . . How can you cash in on this new acceptance of massage? Start up your own small business giving 15-minute mini-massages right where people need it the most—in the office!

Most major cities around the country have massage schools that offer courses that last anywhere from nine months to a year to become a licensed massage therapist. The regulations regarding massage practitioners differ greatly from state to state; California, for example, is more lax about the amount of training needed. A good source of information for what it would take in your state is *Massage* magazine. The back of the magazine lists the rules on a state-by-state basis.

Neck and shoulder massages are traditionally given in a portable massage chair, which is easy to disassemble and take from office to office. It is an odd-looking contraption in which your customer sits and leans forward against a frame with his or her face in a cushioned pillow, leaving the back and shoulders exposed (with clothes on, of course) for you to massage. Massage chairs can cost anywhere from $350 to $600, but massage therapist Nina Foster of La Conner, Washington, suggests looking for a less-expensive used massage chair by checking bulletin boards at massage schools. "The going rate for a 15-minute neck and shoulder massage is between $10 and $15," Foster says. "It can be a nice little extra income for a part-time masseuse."

Finding Clients

The best way to earn significant extra income giving on-site neck and shoulder massages is to approach the office manager of a large office complex. Arrange to come in one day a month with your massage chair and give as many massages (at $10 each) as you can. The office manager can alert the employees as to when you will be there and how much it costs, and possibly even put up a sign-up sheet.

Massage can be physically demanding, but many women who have gone into massage report that they enjoy the nurturing aspect of the work, not to mention the income!

Upholsterer

Dorothy Ferguson's love of antiques led her to learn the art of upholstery. "Such good old wood and solid construction, not at all like the kind of furniture that is built today. Reupholstering an antique chair or sofa is certainly worth doing." And is there a demand for upholstery work? "A big demand," Dorothy says. "I had no problem keeping busy all of the time. Too busy, in fact."

Despite the fact that Dorothy enjoyed what she was doing, she also has stern words of caution for women considering taking up upholstery as a way to earn extra income. "This is a job for strong hands. I was surprised to find out how physical it is, lots of pulling and stretching of the fabric. It is also a pretty good way to get dirty. I had to vacuum my work area all the time!"

It is also not an easy thing to learn. Courses in upholstery are often offered through community skill centers and places like The Learning Exchange, but even after taking a course you should work on your own furniture before hanging out your shingle and taking on paid work. Dorothy herself took a nine-month course at a skill center before hooking up with a local antique store to get clients.

Upholstery requires a heavy-duty sewing machine and small, specialized tools. "You can buy the equipment you need to get started for under $2,000," Dorothy advises. "This is a great way to make money if you love old furniture and take pride in giving something a new life. But it is not something to undertake just for the money."

Thinking It Through

All of the entrepreneurial businesses featured in this chapter have one thing in common—good, honest, physical labor. Kneading knotted neck muscles, reaching for that high outside window under the eaves, or spending an afternoon soaping a fancy car, physical labor can be both financially and spiritually satisfying. Remember one other thing though: You can also get hurt.

To protect your own health and safety and to minimize the potential risk to your clients it is advisable to carry special liability insurance. Many homeowners are wary of hiring unprotected, uninsured entrepreneurs and would never dream of allowing work on their house without proof of insurance. They have very real fears that should an accident occur, they might be sued. Carrying your own coverage is one more selling point that you will have to offer. Ask your insurance agent about what type of coverage would be best, and seek out other entrepreneurs to ask them about the insurance arrangements they recommend. This is an important consideration and should be taken care of before you begin to do any work for others.

In addition to insurance, investigate whether it would be wise to be bonded. I spoke to several weekend entrepreneurs who felt that it was a genuine asset to be able to advertise the fact that they were bonded; it was an important element of their success.

Before you decide to launch one of the "handyperson" businesses described in this chapter, I suggest a trip down to your local hardware store. Neighborhood hardware stores, although they are rapidly disappearing, are great sources of information and research for hardworking extra-income entrepreneurs. There are bulletin boards posted with cards, flyers, and information; check these to see if you will be offering a unique service or if there are already three or four folks in your area who do. Don't stop your research with the bulletin board, engage employees in conversation and you can discover a gold mine of important information: "Thinking of offering a cobweb cleaning service, are ya'? Seems to me that there was a gal around here used to do that but her husband got transferred and she moved away. She did all right, as I recall." Pay attention to the reaction of hardware store employees. If they don't think that a business idea will work in that area, chances are they are right! Save yourself time and money and choose another business.

Introducing yourself to the local hardware clerks will help you with two other things—client referrals and discounts on supplies and equipment. Once the employees are aware of your service and the quality of work that you offer they can be a rich source of business, sending clients your way month after month. And since they know that you are in business and will become a steady hardware store client yourself, you will be able to get tradesman's discounts on the tools and supplies that you purchase.

To learn "back to basics" skills that you do not already know, or to brush up on knowledge you already possess, I recommend investing in the price of the following book:

New Complete Do-It-Yourself Manual
Reader's Digest Books, distributed by Random House
$30

Using back-to-basics skills to make money will serve you well in the long run. These are useful skills to learn, which you can employ for profit when needed and just as easily put to rest when your need for extra income has passed. Basic skills and a willingness to work long and hard are a potentially rewarding combination for any woman.

Chapter Three

Old-Fashioned Money—Look to the Past for Your Financial Future

Why reinvent the wheel every time the tire needs changing? There are many great old-fashioned ways to make extra money in this world, everything from a community bake sale to the standard yard sale. There are also hundreds of services that used to exist and no longer do, goods and services that served a useful purpose but have been abandoned in our rush to embrace the new. Now is the time to reach back and dust a few of those old ideas off and turn them into 21st century sources of additional money! You will also learn about new businesses that use old-fashioned service to take care of brand-new customer needs.

Animal Sitter

With so many busy professionals taking off on business trips on a regular basis, who has time to take care of the dog? Pet sitting is an easy-to-start business that works well for a week-end entrepreneur. "Animal sitting is great for people who have flexible hours," suggests Heather Ireland, owner of Comfy Critters. "I get frequent calls for overnight visits. There are an awful lot of pet owners in this world who don't want their beloved doggy to have to stay alone at night while they are gone. Strange, but true."

Heather charges $25 for staying overnight in her clients' guest room, a great little SAM. Dog walking is another great extra source of cash. Dog walkers charge $8 to $10 an hour and enjoy the extra benefit of exercise for themselves as well as the dog. Heather warns potential dog sitters that you must have free time available both in the mornings and early evenings to take care of most animal care tasks. An additional consideration is that you will be giving up much of your free time during the holidays, the busiest times of the year for animal-sitting services.

Clients can be found a number of ways—flyers distributed on neighborhood doorstops, ads in local papers, information at pet stores and veterinarian offices, and don't forget the best advertisement of all, word-of-mouth recommendations from satisfied customers. It is important that you meet with the owners and their pets (particularly dogs) in the home before you take on sitter responsibilities. The owners will need to show you where the food is kept, where Sissy's favorite bowl is, and the hidden location of the toys and treats.

Not all animals are well-trained or well-behaved, and caution is advised. "This is not a job for fearful people," says Heather. "You need to be extremely comfortable dealing with all kinds of animals; be cautious, but don't ever be fearful."

Animal sitting services are catching on in popularity, so before you try to establish one in your area, scope out possible competition. If there are too many animal sitters in one area or neighborhood, none will be successful. Be very selective about the area; try to find one with a high concentration of professional couples with pure-bred animals. A purr-fect Source of Additional Money for animal lovers!

Antique and Collectibles Dealer

"It started years ago, when I was putting myself through beauty school," Donna Bates said. "I didn't want to go on welfare, so I started buying things at yard sales to resell at the flea market. I graduated to antiques and got interested in costume jewelry as a specialty. After I finished school and started my own shop I just couldn't get rid of the collectibles bug, so now I do it part time." Donna has a stall in an antique mall, she pays $105 a month for her portion, and is required to work there once a month for four hours. It is a perfect setup for a weekend entrepreneur with an interest in antiques or period collectibles. The antique malls and galleries, now spreading coast to coast, are cooperative businesses and the booth operators pitch in to work. The hours that you are required to work will vary according to your booth size; bigger booths may require as many as two days a month.

If you have a real love for antiques and enjoy spending your free time poking around yard sales and flea markets looking for special finds, then this is the SAM for you. Donna Bates' best find ever was a 14-karat gold bracelet and ring for which she paid $2 each! Needless to say, she sold them in her stall for a great deal more. Donna suggests starting by attending estate sales and yard sales to acquire merchandise, and also to acquaint yourself with the local antique market. How to know what is a steal and how to price the bargains that you find? There are handy reference books that list prices on a wide variety of antique and collectible subjects.

Jewelry is very popular among collectors right now, both antique jewelry and collectible pieces from the '20s, '30s, and '40s. "Costume jewelry is much less expensive than the real thing," Donna explained, " and buyers know that old pieces are much better made than what you could buy in a department store now. I also think that people are attracted to the story behind the jewelry. When you buy a piece at Macy's you know that it came straight off of an assembly line somewhere, but when you buy an old piece you can let your imagination run wild about who it once belonged to and what their life was like. Royalty? An impoverished heiress who was forced to sell? You can make up all kinds of stories." In addition to jewelry, many collectors are attracted to fine pieces of china, and Donna observed that large pieces of furniture like dining room sets and bedroom sets seem to move the fastest.

Part-time antiques and collectibles booth dealers divide their free time between scouting for more merchandise and arranging things in their display cases. Once you have developed a reasonable inventory you can spend less time out scouting, but in the beginning it is important to spend both time and money combing your state for merchandise to resell. An established antiques and collectible dealer can have quite a steady little weekend business going!

There are many pricing and reference books on the market to help you determine the retail value of the things you discover in your search. The best and most respected books are published by a company called House of Collectibles.

Beekeeping

Jerry Becker's father began keeping bees in 1919, and Jerry himself has been doing it for the past 30 years. As the Assistant Deputy State Controller for the State of California, Jerry has a very important full-time job, but he finds the time to keep 250 hives scattered around on ranch and farm properties in Northern California. Beekeeping can be very lucrative, and the big money is in renting out hives of bees to orchard owners during the spring.

"Thirty dollars a hive for three weeks, that's what the almond growers will pay," says Jerry. "Cherries and pears, the demand is not as high and the price for a three-week hive rental is only $10 per hive. I know a beekeeper up in Yuba City who keeps 17,000 hives—think about how much he makes during the almond pollination season. Around $510,000 for three weeks!"

In addition to renting his hives to orchards to help Mother Nature pollinate the trees, Jerry sells honey. "I move my hives around seven times a year. After the pollination season is over in Northern California I send my hives down south to the orange groves. The bees' honey is then orange blossom flavored, and that is what I sell to restaurants, cookie manufacturers, and bakeries in bulk. I probably sell about 32,000 pounds of honey a year in 30-pound bulk containers."

Other beekeepers sell their honey in 1-pound jars at flea markets and farmers' market stands. Donald and Pat Hill of San Leandro, California, work several area farmers' markets throughout the year and sell jars of honey as well as handmade beeswax candles. Working just every other weekend, they add anywhere between $6,000 and $15,000 in extra cash to their budget every year! To learn more about beeswax candles, see Chapter 4.

"Working with bees is very satisfying," says Jerry. "You are helping farmers and people raising natural foods, and meeting lots of interesting people. My son is quitting the computer business to go into beekeeping full time!"

In addition to profiting from hive rentals and honey sales, beekeepers can also sell the beeswax to candlemakers like me! Beeswax is used in a vast quantity of products, everything from ski wax to bullet flux. "Royal jelly" is also a premium by-product of beekeeping; it sells in natural food stores for very high prices. A skill that beekeepers can also specialize in is swarm removal: Ordinary folks call you to come and help when a swarm of bees invades their backyard. Removing swarms generally runs about $80, not bad for an afternoon's work!

Beekeeping sounds like a country-based pursuit, but it needn't be. Jerry Becker lives in the midst of a large California town and keeps his hives on farms nearby. "All you need is a cooperative rancher or farmer who has an out-of-the-way patch of land that you can use. I don't pay rent, every Christmas I give them jars of honey, honey candy, and candles."

Most large cities have beekeeping supply stores, just look in the Yellow Pages under *beekeeping*. There are many solid books that will give you an introduction to the craft, among them:

Practical Beekeeping
Enoch Tompkins and Roger M. Griffith
Garden Way Publishing
$9.95
Honey: From Hive to Honeypot
Sue Style
Chronicle Books
$14.95

There are nationwide magazines that serve beekeepers. These magazines are filled with articles and ads that educate and inform their readers about what is going on in the bee business. Mail-order supplies are advertised throughout, so if you don't live near a beekeeping supply store you can discover good sources in the pages of:

Gleanings in Bee Culture
The A.I. Root Company, Publishers
623 W. Liberty St.
Medina, OH 44256
(330) 725-6677

Christmas Bazaars and Open House Craft Boutiques

"Although it always took place the first weekend in October, we would begin meeting with crafters and screening their work in January," Nancy Leneis explained. "My partner and I have always felt that the real key to our success was the high quality that we maintained. Nothing junky or tacky at our Christmas bazaar, that's what keeps our customers coming back every year for seven years!"

The Greenhaven Santa Boutique is an unusual annual bazaar. Crafters each pay $25 to have their goods on display, plus 10% of proceeds. The organizers of the event do very well. "Yes," Nancy laughed, when I pressed her for specifics, "very well." The responsibilities of the bazaar organizers are:

1. Screen potential crafters' work, checking for quality and making sure that the final show does not have any imbalance (four dollmakers and seven tole painters, for instance).

2. Advertise the show extensively. Nancy and her partner kept a mailing list of shoppers from previous years and sent out personal invitations to these folks, inviting them to a special preview time. Ads in newspapers, flyers on telephone poles, and flyers left at other craft shows help attract crowds.

3. Secure a good location and arrange for insurance. "We had our best location in a local school. The school had a bake sale table, so since they were participating we were covered by their insurance policy instead of getting a special one-time rider on our own." Private homes and backyards can work, but gradually the more successful bazaars move to more professional locations.

4. Arrange the goods. "This was the real key to our success and the popularity of the boutique," Nancy explained. "We always had the crafters drop their goods off the night before, and then the show organizers would arrange everything in an appealing way. Instead of just individual crafters sitting behind tables showing off only their own wares, we had several theme rooms in which we built beautiful displays. A Christmas ornament room, a fall holiday room with stuffed pumpkins and turkey things for Thanksgiving and Halloween, a kitchen things room, a pink room, a blue room, and in each room the shoppers would just buy more and more!"

5. Handle the money. "People tend to buy a lot more when they are just writing one big check, and so early on we realized that there should only be one central cashier. As the event organizers, we would handle all of the money and keep track of who sold what. When all of the checks cleared we would total up what each crafter had earned and send them off one check, minus our 10% of course!"

The organizers are also responsible for securing a one-time resale license from the state. Since there is a centralized cashier, the individual crafters are spared the trouble of filling out the sales tax forms. Nancy paid the sales tax before figuring out the individual profits.

"This is a very rewarding and creative way to make money, one of the most rewarding things I've ever done. If you get 20 or 30 crafters together you can really have a big two-day show. The crafters always enjoy our show because they sell so much. One thing to remember is that inexpensive items always sell the best at these events. Make sure that you have a lot of things that are $5 and under. People will buy pricier things, of course, but the cheaper the item, the greater the sales!"

Another variation on what Nancy and her partner did is to create a whole "craft village" in a housing development's model homes. One successful entrepreneur in Northern California arranged just that, and made $60,000 in the course of one weekend! Here's how it works:

Approach the builder or developer of an upscale housing development that still has homes on the market. Tell them that you can bring thousands of people through their model homes in just one weekend; that ought to get their attention fast! The houses themselves should be arranged inside in much the same fashion that Nancy described: Instead of individual booths, the rooms should be filled with artfully arranged merchandise purchased from a central teller. If there are two or three model homes involved you could devote each one to a different theme. Insurance should be less of a problem with this type of event. Talk to the developer about whether the attendees would be covered under their policy. And as for advertising, there is an awfully good chance that the developer will want to help you in a big way. Everybody benefits, you get hoards of customers for the crafts, and the developer gets lots of potential home buyers through its model homes. Remember to take a percentage of your crafters' sales in addition to the participation fee, and you too might be on your way to big weekend bucks.

Custom Gardening

Growing up on a farm in California's Yolo County, Lisa Monckton developed an early love for the land. "My family has been farming the same farm for four generations, from my great-grandfather through to the present generation. On the farm we use modern agricultural techniques, lots of heavy equipment, and chemicals, but over the years my own interests have turned to organic." For many years Lisa and her brother had a restaurant. She went on to become an agricultural inspector. As a hobby she started a large organic vegetable garden in her backyard to supply herself and her friends with tasty fresh produce. Not long after, she founded a part-time custom gardening enterprise called Foodscapes. "The idea just came to me one day while I was fussing with a small onion plant. I thought of all of the people out there who would love to have produce growing outside their back door, but are too timid to get a garden started or don't have the time to establish one. There is a certain mystery to gardens that intimidates people. I realized that I could create a business that puts gardens in for folks."

Lisa grows seedlings at home and then transfers the medium-size plants into her clients' own garden. After first preparing the soil to encourage the plant's proper growth, she places the young plants together in the tightly spaced "French intensive method." A customer can go from dry, weedy, overgrown garden one day to beautifully planted vegetable or flower garden the next, an overnight transformation!

When planting, Lisa follows what she calls the "five Ps" motto: Proper Preparation Prevents Poor Performance. A garden that has been installed by Lisa's methods requires little other than watering by the customer to succeed, delighting her satisfied customers all year 'round with beautiful flowers, culinary and medicinal herbs, and organic produce.

On her initial visit with a client, Lisa quizzes them about which types of plants they would like to grow. "Tomatoes and garlic are by far the most popular requests," she says. But if a customer requests a plant that Lisa does not already have growing in her yard at home, she goes down to the local nursery to purchase it on a "landscaper's discount." Most work is done on the weekends, as many of her clients like to learn alongside Lisa as she works. She plans to add to her businesses services by teaching organic gardening workshops in the future. She also offers organic fertilizers as a side line product.

Lisa's rates for custom gardening are very reasonable— $3 per square foot includes soil preparation, small starter plants, and the actual planting. It is up to the customers to water and pick their produce! Although she feels that a price hike will be in order soon, her price was deliberately low to attract as many first-time clients as possible. "I will have an easier time of it next year when I replant some of my customers' gardens. The soil won't need as much work as it did the first time and I can work much faster." Even though long-time customers' gardens require less care, Lisa's basic price remains the same.

Custom gardening is ideal for extra-income entrepreneurs with a flair for growing. Lisa warns that it is hard and dirty work, but is ultimately rewarding for garden lovers. She tried several standard methods to attract clients—flyers and advertising—with little to no success. "Publicity, that's the best way. I've had an article in the local newspaper and in the city magazine, and both have resulted in clients. As I grow the business I know that I will continue to build upon this base. Repeat business is a terrific moneymaker for me. Organic gardening and organic produce are very hot right now, and I think that things will just continue to get better."

Cut Flowers for Sale

Lee Sturdivant lives on a modest 120-by-180-foot town lot on which she has successfully started a cut flower business to add to her income as a part-time ferry dock attendant. On a typical summer day she walks into her blooming garden with a sharp pair of snips and cuts the following:

> 20 blue delphiniums, retail value $20
>
> 10 mixed bouquets, retail value $40
>
> 40 stems of Sweet William, retail value $7
>
> 2 wedding bouquets, retail value $35
>
> Over $100 in flowers from a garden that will be ready for cutting again the following afternoon!

Flowers are all around us in our lives, and weekend entrepreneurs with skill in the garden are well-placed to profit from the longing to have beautiful fresh flowers decorating a table or sideboard. Anyone with a medium-size garden with good soil and reliable growing seasons can start and maintain a profitable SAM right outside the bedroom window!

To begin a cut flower business, you must first establish your garden. Among the most popular perennial flowers to grow for resale are yarrow, Peruvian lily, columbine, anemone, monkshood, daisies, spirea, bellflower, mums, larkspur, carnations, foxtail lily, baby's breath, lavender, lupine, peonies, oriental poppies, phlox, freesias, lobelia, orchids, ranunculas, spiderwort, and evening primrose.

Perennials usually produce only greenery the first year, waiting until the second year to flower. Growing annuals in your flower garden along with the perennials will allow for a much faster production time. Both annuals and perennials should be started from seeds, the most inexpensive way to get going with your for-profit gardening. Some popular annuals are hollyhocks, snapdragons, bachelor's button, sweet william, dahlias, foxgloves, cosmos, statice, stock, marigolds, and zinnias.

Once your garden is overflowing with mature blossoms you are ready to find customers. Small markets can be approached about carrying your ready-made bouquets; offer to service the in-store display frequently to keep flowers looking fresh and remove unsold bouquets. Farmers' markets are terrific places to sell bouquets, after all, you are a farmer of sorts! Become familiar with the florists in your area; they might be interested in unusual old-fashioned garden flowers in addition to their greenhouse-produced roses. If you live in a well-situated part of town and your garden is visible from the street you might begin to attract private customers who will come to you for fresh flowers for special occasions. Large-scale flower gardens in the country have even been turned into successful "U-pick-It" operations by their owners!

Lee Sturdivant was so pleased by her success as a cut flower grower that she sat down and wrote a detailed book to encourage others to try this business. I highly recommend her book to anyone with a green thumb and an interest in greenbacks!

Flowers for Sale: Growing and Marketing Cut Flowers
Lee Sturdivant
San Juan Naturals
P.O. Box 642
Friday Harbor, WA 98250
$14.95

Office Flower Delivery Service

Georgia Hughes lives in a house on a hill with a flower garden extending down to the street. Filled most of the year with beautiful iris, delphiniums, roses, daisies, and other flowers, Georgia had long been in the habit of bringing bouquets and flower arrangements to work to sit on her desk and remind her of her lovely garden. Her coworkers were also the happy beneficiaries of her garden's largesse. One day it occurred to Georgia that there might be an extra income out there in her yard. For many years there has been a movement among small farmers called "community-sustained agriculture" whereby a farmer sells his or her produce in advance to a group of families and supplies them with weekly deliveries of fresh produce. "Why not apply the same concept to fresh flowers?" Georgia thought, and promptly organized a weekly bouquet delivery service.

Her customers receive weekly arrangements of fresh flowers, whatever flowers happen to be blooming that week. Customers commit in advance to a three-month service, and pay $10 weekly for the flowers. She is still building her customer list, but looks forward to earning an extra $50 to $100 a week from an old hobby she has long cultivated.

Finding Clients

"I started with the woman in the cubicle next to mine," Georgia says, "and it started to spread by word of mouth from there." She plans to have flyers made up to distribute to other businesses that have large staffs. "The best way to do this would be to build a route that involved several deliveries at just a few big office buildings. My goal is to have ten weekly clients in just two buildings!"

Another good resource book for starting a flower-related business is:

Plants for Sale
Melanie Harrison
Kangaroo Press
(513) 381-3881
$10.95

And for ideas on what to grow and how to grow it:

Cutting Gardens: The Complete Guide to Growing Flowers and Creating Special Arrangements for Every Season and Every Region
Anne Halpin and Betty Mackey
Simon and Schuster
$27.50

Foraging the Wild for Profit

Like our pioneer ancestors before us, it is still possible to forage in the wild. Instead of foraging for wood to keep us warm and berries to keep us fed, we can forage for profit! No matter what part of the country you live in, things are growing near your neighborhood that can be picked for free and sold for a terrific profit, or else used as an element in a craft project that you can sell for a wonderful SAM. *The Wall Street Journal* recently featured Oregon lumberjacks who forage pine cones to add to their bottom line. Most small pine cones sell for 25¢, and some large pine cones sell for as much as $12 apiece in Japan. On a recent trip from California up through Oregon and Washington I constantly turned my head to see wildflowers, beautiful autumn leaves, flowering sage brush, pine cones, and evergreens lining the back roads just waiting to be harvested by an enterprising weekend entrepreneur. A half-hour hike in the woods with my husband yielded an abundance of small hemlock cones and a good supply of lichen (or goat's beard). Two hours of work with a needle and thread and a $4 grapevine wreath form combined with my foraged materials produced a beautiful "Pacific Northwest Christmas" wreath, which I sold a few weeks later at a craft fair for $30. A few minutes of picking bunches of wild straw flowers from the side of the road on a mountainside near Ashland, Oregon, also brought a tidy profit when I bound individual bunches with ribbon and sold them at my candle booth for $1 a bunch. At the same craft fair I also sold small bunches of heavenly scented eucalyptus leaves (which I harvested from a tree in my own backyard) for $2 a bunch. The only extra touch I added to my foraged greens and flowers were small satin ribbons to bind the ends and give them a more finished look. I added an extra $60 of pure profit, just by taking a walk in the woods. Thank you, Mother Nature!

Among the things that can be foraged in the wild for your financial benefit are: acorns, mistletoe, moss and lichen, wild mushrooms, berries, wildflowers, autumn leaves, evergreen branches and boughs, pine cones, thistles and teazels, fallen wood, dried grasses, pussy willows, wild roses, heather, holly, eucalyptus, manzanita, rocks and pebbles, seedpods, cattails, wheat, pine needles, owl pellets, and mugwhort.

Many of the things that you pick up on hikes and walks in nature can be used in hand-crafted projects like wreaths, woven baskets, swags, and decorative hangings. Christmas is an especially good time to forage to your advantage—Christmas gift boutiques, tree lots, and craft fairs abound and are the perfect place to sell your wares. If you really dedicate yourself to developing a reputation for quality work and original creations, the catalog market is worth trying. Flipping through a selection of high quality national mail-order catalogs filled with holiday merchandise I saw countless products that were made from materials that could have been foraged for free from a nearby forest, field, or meadow. Among the high-ticket items that an enterprising weekend entrepreneur could make from free materials were:

> Eucalyptus wreath (eucalyptus leaves layered in a fish-scale pattern and secured by bronze boat nails) $46
>
> Alpine wreath (made from white larkspur, California lace moss, salal and melaleuca leaves, saracenia lilies, brunia, sage, and pine cones woven on a base of huckleberry vine) $69
>
> Pine cone tree (clusters of pine cones joined to form a rustic tree) $18
>
> Winter woodland wreath (cedar, oak leaves, salal, sweet Annie, ferns, and boxwood accented with hazelnuts, lotus pods, and large white roses) $56
>
> Summer spray (field-dried grasses, sunflowers, roses, bay and malaleuca leaves, blue larkspur, bound with raffia) $52

Fresh holly wreath (freshly picked Oregon holly leaves and berries) $36

Harvest garland (oak leaves, bay, pepperberries, peppergrass, and marjoram tied with raffia) $46

Mistletoe and eucalyptus kissing ball $23

Two-pound bag of scented pine cones $13.50

Pine cone door hanger $16

Pine cone wreath (traditional wreath made from pine cones ornamented with kitchen spices—orange peel, cinnamon, assorted nuts, and star anise) $69

Fragrant pomander balls $4.95

Fall colors wreath (oak leaves, eucalyptus, bay laurel, white California moss, seedpods, bittersweet) $59

Preserved autumn leaves $9.95

The best foraged item of all in one of the catalogs: rocks that had been painted to look like cats. "Water-shaped through the ages, gathered from Appalachian creeks, hand-painted, signed, and dated by the artist. Terrific gift for people who love cats, rocks, or pets, or anyone who uses paperweights! Each pet is about 5 inches long, weighs up to one pound and no two are alike," the catalog description read. These painted rocks sold for $17.50 each. I hope you are starting to get the idea that a lot can be done with what nature provides!

To learn more about how to craft wreaths and dried floral arrangements from foraged materials, I recommend several books at the end of this section. Other than producing crafts or seasonal items from nature, another steady source of customers for your foraging discoveries is florists.

Gardening is the "sport of the '90s" and high-end gardening stores are opening up all over. These stores are potential customers for well-made items from foraged materials.

In addition to the front-page story about foraging loggers that appeared in *The Wall Street Journal,* the very same business newspaper also featured a lengthy story on foraging for owl pellets (owl regurgitations), which are sought after for use in high school biology classes. It is no longer politically correct to dissect frogs, and owl pellets are chock full of tiny mouse bones and snake skins guaranteed to intrigue budding scientists. Scientific supply houses pay top dollar for owl pellets, and successful pellet foragers are very secretive about which old dusty barns hold their fortunes.

When foraging in the wild, there are a few rules to keep in mind. The first, and most important, is to research your finds. Always know what you have collected and whether or not it is safe. Wild mushrooms in particular are very dangerous and should never be collected and sold unless you are familiar with all of the varieties. Mushrooming courses are sometimes available in areas where wild mushrooms grow, and there are numerous local mushroom collecting societies that you can join to learn more about it. If you establish yourself as a wild mushroom forager with a good reputation for safe mushrooms you can develop a devoted clientele among gourmet restaurants.

The other rule to keep in mind is that, despite the fact that so much of what grows in nature seems like it should be available for us to take, it is not. Before collecting wild flowers, grasses, or anything else from the side of a highway, check with the highway patrol to see if this is legal. Be sensitive to private property and respect the rights of others. Do not attempt to forage on land that you suspect may be privately owned without first checking with the owner. And remember that it is illegal to remove anything from a national park or forest.

Stern warnings aside, I encourage you to look at the world around you in a whole new way. Once you start to see the potential products or materials waiting for an enthusiastic weekend entrepreneur (and her helpful family!) to scoop them up, you will be astonished at what nature provides. Get busy!

Here are useful books about foraging and crafting from foraged materials:

Taming the Wild Mushroom: A Culinary Guide to Foraging
Arleen and Alan Bessette
University of Texas Press
$24.95

All That the Rain Promises, and More . . .
A Hip Pocket Guide to Western Mushrooms
David Arora
Ten Speed Press
$17.95

Mushroom: The Journal of Wild Mushrooming
P.O. Box 3156
Moscow, ID, 83843
$15 per year

Herbal Wreaths: More than 60 Fragrant, Colorful
Wreaths to Make and Enjoy
Carol Taylor
Sterling/Lark
$27.95

The Complete Book of Nature Crafts: How to Make
Wreaths, Dried Flowers Arrangements, Potpourris, Dolls,
Baskets, Gifts, Decorative Accessories for the Home, and
Much More
Eric Carlson, Dawn Cusick, and Carol Taylor
Rodale Press
$27.95

Year-Round Wreaths: Creative Ideas for Every Season
Richard Kollath
Facts-on-File
$21.95

Baskets from Nature's Bounty
Elizabeth Jensen
Interweave Press
$24.95

Garage Sales and Yard Sales

For weeks I'd been carefully saving money for an autumn trip
to the Pacific Northwest. I was pleased with the size of my
savings account and congratulated myself on a job well done,

until my car suddenly needed several hundred dollars in emergency repairs! Overnight the vacation money that I'd squirreled away was gone. Rather than cancel a trip I was looking forward to I decided that an emergency SAM was needed—a garage sale!

Nothing can beat a yard sale or garage sale for instant cash. Look around your house, poke around in the garage, peer into the back of your closet, and I am certain that you will discover many things you once needed but haven't used in years. "Gee, do I really need my scuba weight belt? I haven't been diving since 1990! And these bags of cassette tapes, when did I last listen to Men at Work?" I was ruthless in my appraisal of what should stay and what should go, and after only two hours I had collected an impressive array of goods. On to the next step—having the sale.

Newspaper advertising always pays off for a yard sale. Your best customers will be early birds (who we now know are in fact weekend entrepreneurs out scouting for super deals on things that they can resell at their flea market booth or refurbish and sell at an antique mall) who arrive close to dawn to peer at your goods. Throughout the day you will notice carloads of people consulting the classified ads, the $20 or so that you spend on a garage sale ad brings in much greater customer traffic.

To make your sale look larger and therefore more visually enticing to passersby, ask your friends and invite them to bring extra things over to sell. Just about everyone has a few things sitting around that they no longer need, and they would be happy to let you sell them for a small percentage. When they stop by to deliver their things, don't be too surprised if they buy something of yours before they leave!

The evening before your sale is a great time to sort through things and price all of the items. This should all be done beforehand; once your sale gets going you will not have time to pay attention to these small details. Decide which priced items you will remain firm on, and which items you will be willing to bargain lower to get out of your garage for good!

Make sure that you have at least $20 in small bills on hand, and a few dollars' worth of change.

The morning of your sale, get up very, very early. This is a key element to yard sale success; posters and signs must be posted around the neighborhood before 8:00 A.M. in order to really draw. Make sure that your signs clearly point the way to your house, and that they arc readable from a distance. During the course of the day it is a good idea to send a friend or spouse around to check up on your signs and make sure that they are still posted.

The actual sale will go by very quickly. Time seems to fly as more and more people mingle around on your front lawn asking about prices, checking over bargains, and then handing you crisp green dollars. Few things are as satisfying as the ever-growing wad of dollar bills in your jeans pocket on the day of a garage sale. At the end of the day I drag the leftovers back into the garage to await the next sale, and I carefully remove my signs from the neighborhood telephone poles. Time to rest and count my money!

Here are the steps to a successful yard or garage sale:

Beforehand

1. Choose your date and place your ads.
2. Select items and begin pricing.
3. Make large signs for the neighborhood.
4. Get quarters, dimes, nickels, and single bills for change.

The Day of the Sale

1. Get up very early and put signs out.
2. Haul stuff onto front lawn or driveway.
3. Enjoy the action!

A great resource book on successful garage sales is:

The Fabulous Money-Making Garage Sale Kit
Sourcebooks, Inc.
$12.95

Herb Farming

America is wild about fresh herbs, and small-time herb farming is an ideal business for an extra-income entrepreneur. Using just your own backyard (or in some cases your own basement or garage) it is possible to grow enough herbs to generate a SAM that produces an extra $50 to $250 a week. Gives a whole new slant to the expression "growing a business"!

There are plenty of ways to make money with the herbs you grow.

1. Sell them wholesale to small local grocery stores and specialty food markets that would like to offer a good selection of fine organic, locally grown herbs to their customers. As more mainstream cooks begin to use herbs, even grocery stores who traditionally stock only parsley are beginning to branch out into basil, dill, and cilantro.

2. Sell direct to the customer at retail prices at farmers' markets and roadside stands. In addition to selling cut herbs for cooking, you might also offer small potted herb plants. Dried herb packets, potpourris, herbal vinegars, sachets, and mixed herb and flower bouquets are a few other products you could sell at your stall.

3. Restaurants who specialize in gourmet dishes are a ready market for your locally grown herbs. Approach the chef and offer a steady supply of high-quality, "just-picked" herbs and you will make a friend for life. Bakers add herbs to breads and rolls and are potential wholesale customers.

4. Herbalists and aromatherapists are emerging everywhere. Fresh herbs are a critical part of what they offer. Acquaint yourself with the field and find out which herbs would be of most use to them.

5. Caterers can be a steady source of business. Catering is a competitive business and canny caterers are always looking for ways to distinguish themselves from their competition. Why not convince a few that they can have the freshest herbs around?

6. Herbs are sometimes used in teas, most notably chamomile. Offering dried chamomile tea, either for drinking or as a hair rinse, is an ideal side product to fresh culinary herbs.

7. Mail-order sales of potted plants and unusual seeds can be a potential source of revenue once you have a well-established herb garden. This requires a space larger than the average backyard, however.

8. Herbal cosmetics are gaining in popularity once again (in times past they were the only kind available!). You can research and develop your own herbal cosmetic products to sell retail, or contact herbal cosmetics companies about wholesale sales of your fresh herbs.

As you can see, herbs have unlimited potential as a cash crop and are easy to get started right away. I spoke to Lee Sturdivant of San Juan Naturals in Friday Harbor, Washington, about how she got started as an herb grower: "I started growing herbs for my own kitchen, and began giving the overflow away to friends. It was a short step from supplying friends for free to supplying local restaurants for profit! Like lettuce, fresher is better when it comes to herbs. Local restaurants and grocery stores prefer buying from local growers because, not only is it very fresh, but they don't have to pay shipping costs. Growing herbs is definitely a great way to be a weekend entrepreneur. Because of the growing cycle you don't have to commit yourself to a year-round business."

There are many culinary herb varieties, but not all are popular with cooks. The best herbs to grow now are basil, dill, French tarragon, mint, oregano, rosemary, chives, parsley, and thyme.

Herb farmers have a built-in audience, and many businesses with a need for herbs, such as restaurants, bakers, and herbalists, prefer dealing with a local producer. Danuta Lake, an herbalist in Anacortes, Washington, told me that she really likes buying herbs from local growers for her business, Sun Moon Botanicals. "I like knowing where the herbs come from and the conditions under which they were grown. I also like to support other local people." She recommends that small-time herb growers stick to the basic European herb varieties since there is the greatest need for them. Don't be afraid or intimidated about approaching these folks for business, because they will be pleased to know that you grow herbs they can use.

Fresh Catnip Products

While researching this chapter, I became entranced with herbs and the vast number of products that can be developed from your own crop. Catnip toys, even! Grow catnip and sew it inside of cute fabric toys that you can either sell yourself as a sideline or offer to local pet stores on a wholesale basis. The fresher the catnip the more the cat loves it, so the pet store would actually be offering their customers a superior product. Try it and tell me how it goes!

Herb Topiaries

Upscale catalogs for cooks and gardeners have lately started to sell high-priced topiaries (shaped plants) made from herbs. In a recent Smith & Hawken gardening catalog, a topiary plant made from thyme and sold in a simple 4-inch terra cotta clay pot retailed for $19, and a potted rosemary topiary was $35. *Martha Stewart Living* magazine also featured a photo of dainty little herb topiary in china tea cups; just think how popular that would be at a craft sale! Anyone with a green thumb can grow herb plants, and learn how to shape the plant as it grows so that it achieves a nice round look. There is a market for herb topiary, not just at farmers' markets and weekend craft fairs, but at the nurseries and plant stores in your neighborhood. The following book is a good basic primer on topiary in general, with a chapter on creating herb topiary:

> *The Complete Book of Topiary*
> Barbara Gallup and Deborah Reich
> Workman Publishing
> $13.95

Info on herb topiary can also be found in a great book I mention often:

> *Gifts from the Herb Garden*
> Emelie Tolley and Chris Mead
> Clarkson Potter
> $20

Dried Flower Topiary

Once you get interested in herb topiary you will learn that, in addition to growing topiaries, you can craft them out of dried flowers. Dried rosebuds make beautiful topiary bushes. When decorated with ribbon and placed into gold-painted pots, dried flower topiaries are a popular item at weekend craft fairs. Here is a book to help you learn how to make dried flower topiaries to sell for extra income:

> *The Complete Book of Dried Topiaries: A Step-by-Step Guide to Creating 25 Stunning Arrangements*
> Carol Endler Sterbenz
> Courage Books
> $21.95

Growing herbs is not difficult, and there are several good books available to help you develop skills. Look in your local bookstore or library for the following titles:

> *Step-by-Step Herbs*
> Better Homes and Gardens
> $12.95

> *Little Herb Gardens: Simple Secrets for Glorious Gardens*
> Georgeanne Brennan and Mimi Luebbermann
> Chronicle Books
> $12.95

In addition to books about growing herbs, several books are now available to help you with the business of selling herbs.

> *Pay Dirt: How to Raise and Sell Specialty Herbs and Vegetables for Serious Cash*
> Mimi Luebbermann
> Prima Publishing
> $13

> *Profits from Your Backyard Herb Garden*
> Lee Sturdivant
> San Juan Naturals
> Box 642
> Friday Harbor, WA 98250
> $10.95

Backyard Cash Crops: The Sourcebook for Growing and Marketing Specialty Plants
Craig Wallin
Homestead Design, Inc.
P.O. Box 1058
Bellingham, WA 98227
$16.95

As more people take up herb farming as a business or a hobby, more publications devoted to herbs seem to appear. The best magazine is *The Herb Companion*. It is filled with articles of interest to herb growers and herb fanciers, and includes lots of information and advertising from a variety of seed and plant sources. In addition to magazines sold on newsstands, several newsletters are available that cater to the business of herb growing. These newsletters are filled with valuable information on marketing and selling herbs:

Specialty Crop Digest
Homestead Design, Inc.
P.O. Box 1058
Bellingham, WA 98227

The Business of Herbs
Northwind Farm
Route 2, Box 246G
Shevlin, MN 56676

The Herb Growing and Marketing Network
publishers of both *The Herbal Connection*
and *The Herbal Green Pages*
For information, call (717) 393-3295

Growing Ginseng

One unusual plant with spectacular financial possibilities is ginseng, a medicinal herb. Long sought after in Asia, cultivated ginseng is now grown in some parts of the U.S. The price per pound varies from year to year and depends on the quality and type of ginseng root, but can be anywhere from $30 to $150. That's right, $150 a pound, but it is a long-term investment that can take eight to ten years before your first crop comes in. Last year the total cultivated ginseng exported from the United States was 1,289,000 pounds, valued at $62 million. With the growing interest in alternative medicine and healing, both in America and abroad, this market is certain to expand. To learn more about ginseng and whether it can be grown in your area, write for information to:

Buckhorn Ginseng
Route 4, Box 336
Richland Center, WI 53581

Raising Goats and Sheep

Do you live in the country? If you do, you might have noticed how some of your neighbors are earning extra money by raising goats and sheep. Goats can be raised either for milk or for meat. "Americans are slowly coming around to eating goat meat. There is a big ethnic market for it in the Greek and Hispanic communities," Dana Hixson told me. "And goat cheese has been very popular for the last ten years or so."

To raise goats you must have access to several acres of irrigated land with a strong fence. "Goats will get under, over, or around a fence if it is not strong enough. A good fence is really an important element for success," advises Dana, after years of experience. You can sustain 7.5 goats per irrigated acre. Goats do not graze on natural grasses, but rather eat broadleaf or treefoil clover, or perennial orchard grass, all of which must be planted. Raising livestock can take a little or a lot of time, depending on the season. Dana describes her life during the late winter/early spring birthing season as being "on call 24 hours a day," but the rest of the year she spends just a few hours each day doing goat-related chores.

Don't think you could stomach raising little goats and then shipping them off to the meat market? You might be better suited to raising sheep for wool. Longtime avid weaver and country living enthusiast Mary Cutting turned her hobby into a part-time moneymaker when she began raising sheep and selling the shorn wool to weavers.

"You can raise one sheep per acre of land. Sheep do eat the natural grasses, but if you want more that one sheep on an acre you can supplement their feed with grain and other store-bought supplies. From a money-making standpoint though, the quantity of sheep you raise is less important than the quality of the wool they produce." The most salable product is pure white wool, a fact Mary did not learn until after her first season. "I went with my own personal taste, which is more towards natural colors. But white wool sells much better than black, brown, or gray. Now I know!"

Shearing sheep is a skill and an art, and Mary recommends hiring a professional to do the job. But once the wool is shorn, it is up to you to market it. To find customers for her wool Mary went straight to weavers and spinners themselves. "This is definitely a specialty market, and your product must be acceptable." High-quality wool can bring anywhere from $2 to $10 a pound. "And if you can't find any other customers, Pendleton pays 50¢ a pound," Mary laughs.

For a good source of books on raising small livestock, call this bookstore in Davis, California:

Ag Access
(916) 756-7177

They will happily recommend books and ship them out to you.

Pet Food Delivery Service

As the pace of life speeds up, there are so many promises that go unkept . . . like the vow you took to feed your animals only that nutritionally sound pet food that requires a special trip to the vet's office to buy. Sometimes you remember, but all too often Fido and Sissy eat whatever you managed to pluck off the shelf at the neighborhood grocery. But what if someone would bring that fancy pet food right to your door whenever you needed it? What a great idea!

Kristine Backus owns Pet Meals on Wheels, and that is the exact service that she provides. While working part time as the head of the computer lab in an elementary school, she spends several hours a week driving her pickup truck filled with Science Diet, Iams, Nutro, and other superior pet food brands to service her 250 regular customers. She delivers a minimum of 20 pounds of food at a time, and instead of charging for delivery, she merely marks up the price of the food. Her dog Kitzy accompanies her on her route, adding to the laid-back and "stress-free" nature of her business.

Most of her customers are affluent people who are short on time but long on ideas about how their lives should be: only the best for these folks and their pets. Word-of-mouth, flyers dropped on doorsteps or given out in veterinarian offices (only offices that don't already sell food!), and networking with local pet-sitters and dog groomers have brought clients her way. "Find a neighborhood filled with lots of houses and blanket the area with flyers. I go out and do it on my roller skates!" Kristine says. "That way you can pick up several clients in the same neighborhood and have a more efficient route."

Delivering pet food is a business for animal lovers and people who genuinely care about animals' health and happiness. You will need to educate yourself on the upscale brands available and the relative advantages of each brand. It is also important to educate yourself about the competition: How much do local pet food stores charge for the brands that you will be offering? Find pet food wholesalers in your area by looking in the business-to-business phone directories, and keep in mind that some of the retail stores themselves might be willing to sell to you at wholesale if your orders are large enough.

Real Estate Agent's Helper

Real estate agents can't be everywhere at once, no matter how hard they try. Holding open houses, showing property, meeting with lenders, and prospecting for new clients—it's a nonstop job. To do a more efficient job it is common for real estate agents to hire freelance assistants to help them with some of the less technical parts of their work.

"Open House" signs sprout like mushrooms on the weekends and every one of those signs symbolizes a potential opportunity for a SAM. "I hire an assistant to help me with an open house on an average of once a month," says Margaret Greenberg, "whenever I have more than one home that I am trying to market. I work one open house, and the assistant works the other. The job is very simple—just greet folks as they enter and hand them a brochure about the house. Because the assistant is not a licensed real estate agent themselves, they cannot answer questions, but spend the entire afternoon saying, 'I can have the listing agent call you to answer that question.' It's a pretty simple way to make money on a weekend." Margaret pays her assistants $30 for three hours. Sure sounds easy, but how can one find work as a freelance real estate agent's helper? Start with any real estate agents that you might know. Suggest to them that their time is more profitably spent on activities other than holding homes open on weekend afternoons. As Margaret Greenberg sums it up, "An agent's time is most profitably spent prospecting. Open houses are too slow. It is just not efficient. I could be making contact with 50 potential prospects on the phone in an afternoon instead of standing in an open house meeting five." Remind the agents that you can help increase their efficiency and effectiveness. If you do not know any real estate agents personally, make it a point to stop in and meet them when they are holding open houses! There they are, just waiting for you to offer to help.

In addition to holding open houses, there are a number of other nonprofessional tasks that you could offer to perform for real estate agents: dropping off brochures and flyers, helping with holiday promotions (many agents like to distribute flags on July 4th), and if you have computer skills, helping with newsletters. Telemarketing for real estate agents is another possibility, cold-calling for prospects. All these tasks are such that they can easily be done during available hours.

Important things to remember about working as a real estate agent's assistant:

1. Appearance—you must be neat, clean, and professionally dressed. Suit and tie for men, business suit or dress for women.

2. Speech—you must be well spoken and able to communicate easily with strangers.

3. Manners—you must be well-mannered and polite at all times.

4. Promptness and reliability—you must be on time. If an agent needs you at noon, be there!

5. Professionalism—remember that you are not a licensed real estate agent and cannot talk about price or terms. Do not attempt to answer technical questions or you and your agent will be on dangerous legal ground. Please check into the restrictions and regulations that apply in your state.

Concierge Service

A concierge? Those haughty people in fancy hotels that look down their noses at you when you ask for a restaurant recommendation? No, not exactly. Nowadays the term "concierge" is used to describe someone who runs an errand and odd-job service to help busy professionals. Latter-day concierges, for a fee, will stand in line at the Department of Motor Vehicles, pick up dry cleaning, and even find out which is the best day-care center in the neighborhood. In New York a woman named Gloria Newman operates her business under the name, Your Own Personal Concierge; while in Philadelphia, Molly Hanford runs More Than Just Errands. Both provide essentially the same services for busy people: They make their money by taking care of time-consuming, irritating chores that no one else does willingly.

Personal concierges will do just about anything that is legal, and charge fees ranging from $20 to $60 an hour. Some even organize! Rent-a-Mom of Reston, Virginia, will come in and organize closets and drawers for a minimum of $60.

Finding Clients

How do personal concierges find their clients? Start off inexpensively by sending a press release about your services to the local business newspaper or magazine. They are always looking for human interest stories of interest to their business readers, and a service like yours will be ideal for their audience. Make up a professional flyer that lists your fees and services, and stick it under the windshield wipers of every expensive foreign car you see parked in a hospital lot! Or try large office buildings filled with lawyers and other well-paid and overworked professionals.

Dry Cleaning Service

Although the personal concierge service described above will do just about anything legal, a clever entrepreneur in San Francisco has taken the same time-saving concept and applied it to just one type of service—dry cleaning. David Chin set up a folding card table in the underground parking lot of a large office building and began taking in clothes that office workers needed to have dry cleaned but wanted to spare themselves the hassle of taking it to the cleaners themselves. He does not do the actual dry cleaning himself, but rather takes it all to a commercial laundry where he has negotiated a lower rate (so that his profit is higher). Two or three days later he personally delivers the dry-cleaned shirts, suits, and skirts directly to the owner's office. The door-to-door service costs about the same as the premium price at an upscale dry cleaners: $1.80 per shirt, $9.50 per suit, and Chin's overworked customers are happy to pay it.

To establish a business like David Chin's Park 'N' Dry, you will need to find a large office building that caters to professionals and convince its management to let you offer this service to tenants and their employees. Offering to pay a small rent on a portion of their garage should work; it is space that would otherwise sit idle and not earn rent.

Child Care for Sick Kids

How can I write a book on extra-income opportunities for women and not mention the oldest (almost) way of all—baby-sitting?

But baby-sitting with a twist, updated for today's life. According to a national day-care association, there is a huge unmet need for sick child care. No doubt you have encountered this need yourself! Each day there are more than 350,000 children under 14 (with both parents working) who are too sick to attend school or child care. As you know, the minute your child has a runny nose or a fever your day-care provider doesn't want your child anywhere near! This creates a big need for a service that provides occasional day care for sick children, either in your home or the child's home.

How can you let working parents know that you are available to take care of their sick child? Start by sending information out to the day-care providers in your area; they should be happy to pass your name along to desperate parents who need your help. Contacting the local parents' newspaper will also give you a start, either through advertising or possibly an article about your unusual service.

How much to charge? Find out what the going day rate is at local day-care centers then add a bit of a premium, say an extra $10.

The best background for this sort of baby-sitting service would be a nursing background, but at the very least you should have current CPR and other emergency life-saving training to help parents feel at ease.

Hotel Restaurant Child Care for "Parent's Night Out"

I hope that this is the start of a nationwide trend—twice in the past month I have noticed hotel restaurants that offer free baby-sitting service for their diners. The Hyatt Regency in Hilton Head, South Carolina, and also a lovely hotel here in my own neighborhood, the Rocklin Park Hotel. The Rocklin Park Hotel offers "child-care night" twice a month. Local parents (or hotel guests) come with their children in tow and pass them into the care of a hotel baby-sitter who has set up one of the rooms with kids' videos and toys. What a terrific idea. "We offer it from 6:00 P.M. to 9:00 P.M., so some couples come right at 6:00 and stay until 9:00! They bring books, magazines, bills that need paying, or they use the time to just talk to each other," an employee told me.

How can you set up a service like this in your area? Approach the manager of a large hotel that also has an upscale dining room. Once you outline the idea to the manager, he or she should understand what an enormous boon it would be to the restaurant's dinner business. It is also a great opportunity for the establishment to garner some positive publicity! The Rocklin Park Hotel posts a large notice in its entryway to let lunch and dinner patrons know when the next "child-care night" is scheduled. No real advertising is necessary, so the only cost to the hotel will be the price that you negotiate for your time. Point out to the management that the benefits to the hotel would far outweigh the cost of paying you.

Scented Geraniums

Dawn Hardy tried many different methods of making an extra income before finding one that has not only touched her heart, but has turned out to be quite lucrative as well. "I tried everything," she told me, "from writing books to selling beaded jewelry to writing catalog copy for a big company here in town, but nothing really clicked for me. And then one day I was helping a friend weed her herb garden. There were these scented geraniums that were just going to be pulled out and tossed on the trash heap, but I asked if I could have them and try to replant them at my house. And lo and behold, not only did they thrive at my house, I have developed quite a tidy little business growing and selling scented geraniums."

Scented geraniums are considered an herb, one with both culinary and medicinal uses. Dawn now grows 120 different varieties (there are close to 300), everything from apple-scented to a nutmeg-scented variety. She sells her plants at local farmers' markets, charging $3 for a 3-inch pot and up to $25 for a large hanging basket. She has also approached plant stores and sells them scented geraniums wholesale. Dawn has developed her extra-income business to the point that her husband is considering quitting his job to join her business!

To learn more about the history of scented geraniums and how to grow them successfully, Dawn recommends the following book:

Scented Geraniums
Jim Becker and Faye Brawner
Interweave Press
$12.95

A wholesale source of scented geranium seedling:

Herb Heaven
P.O. Box 2066
Sandpoint, ID 83864

Thinking It Through

Many of the ideas in this section are no-brainers, simple one-shot ideas like yard sales, but others are more complicated and time-consuming. Before embarking on a business like custom gardening or beekeeping, think long and hard about your lifestyle and your own commitment to creating a successful extra-income opportunity.

Time is important to all of us, and we value the free time spent planted on the couch with the remote control in one hand and a big bag of popcorn in the other. Some of these old-fashioned ideas require large investments of time to achieve success, so please be realistic about how much of your time you are willing to devote. No sense spending money on bee-hives or planting an herb patch in the backyard if ultimately you decide that it is too time-consuming to pursue. Sit down and do an honest evaluation of how much time you will be willing to spend and make sure that you choose a Source of Additional Money that fits that mold. Also examine your immediate cash needs. Can you afford to wait until a crop grows to maturity or bees produce their honey? If your landlord is banging on your door for the rent or you have to pay for your son's braces now, a yard sale is a better SAM than gourmet vinegars. Once you take care of the immediate cash crunch then perhaps you can turn your attention to an entrepreneurial enterprise with a more long-term payoff.

Remember, there are many more old-fashioned ways to make extra money than the ideas presented here. Think back to your childhood, or stories that your parents and grandparents told about the way "life used to be." Can you think of a successful business that seems to have disappeared over the years for no apparent reason? Let history be your guide, and you may well discover an old-time gold mine!

Chapter Four

Crafty Business—
Money-Making Ideas
for Craft Fairs

Crafts and hobbies have kept many of us happy and busy throughout the years. With the crafts craze sweeping the nation, selling the crafts we make can also keep us happily going to the bank to make hefty deposits! Detailed in this chapter are exciting ways to make money selling crafts at fairs, bazaars, boutiques, and markets, as well as through mail-order catalogs, gift shops, and department stores. If you already make crafts now, think about kicking your hobby into a higher gear and turning it into an extra-income opportunity. If you don't have a craft or hobby already, take a look at some of the options here, choose one, and start making money as fast as you can make your products!

Bird Houses and Bird Feeders

You may have read that Americans are going through a phase called "nesting" where instead of going out on the town in pursuit of pleasure they are staying put on the couch watching videos and reading books, working around the house, and just generally enjoying the quiet life. This "nesting" movement has also inspired an interest in our feathered friends, wild birds. Nature walks to observe birds are a big deal, sales of binoculars and field guides are way up, and everyone wants a beautiful custom-made bird house or bird feeder hanging outside their window. This is an ideal time to put your woodworking and designing skills to work and start your own weekend bird house business.

Bird houses and bird feeders come in all sizes, shapes, and materials. Some entrepreneurs make them from recycled scrap wood, others use foraged materials from the woods to create a more outdoorsy look. One Northern California crafter covers the exteriors of her handmade bird houses with the seedpods from pine cones. A popular design technique is to custom-build a birdhouse that is a miniature copy of the homeowner's own abode, even painted to match!

There are many ways to market hand-crafted bird houses and bird feeders. Craft fairs are the natural place to start, but keep in mind that most folks who shop at craft fairs like items in the under-$5 range. During one afternoon craft fair I hung up a Frank Lloyd Wright-inspired bird feeder that my husband Peter built; at $60 it had plenty of admirers but no actual purchasers. If you plan to sell your wares at a craft fair it is best to experiment with fairly simple designs that you can sell cheaply and still make a profit. To sell high-priced bird houses and feeders a better method is to approach the merchandise buyer at one of the many nature or outdoor-themed stores cropping up all over. Offer your product to the store at a wholesale price (approximately 50% of what you think it will sell for retail) or ask if they will handle it on consignment. With a consignment arrangement you will be paid only when the bird feeder sells, but you can expect to keep a little more than 50%. Ambitious woodworkers with more capital to invest might try advertising their custom bird houses or feeders in regional lifestyle magazines like *Sunset* or *Southern Living,* but the cost of display advertising is high and this is a risky method for a beginner.

Once you begin building bird houses and bird feeders you will find that your designs will become more and more imaginative, but to get started with ideas you might take a look at these two books:

The Bird House Book: How to Build Fanciful Bird Houses and Feeders, from the Purely Practical to the Absolutely Outrageous
Bruce Woods and David Schoonmaker
Sterling/Lark
$14.95

The Bird Feeder Book: How to Build Unique Bird Feeders, from the Purely Practical to the Simply Outrageous
Thom Boswell
Sterling/Lark
$24.95

Cats and Kittens

We all love our pets, and cat-lovers sometimes seem to be the most devoted of all. Not only do they lavish love and attention on their cats, but they also spend big bucks on cat and kitten-themed merchandise. There are retail stores around the country that carry nothing but items for cat fanciers. Weekend entrepreneurs might find making cat-related crafts a purr-fect way to make extra money!

Crafters can make a wide variety of cat- and kitten-inspired merchandise. Quilted cat dolls dressed in clothing, needlepoint and embroidered wall hangings, painted wood or stone doorstops (take a look at the foraging section for a great idea here!), T-shirts and sweatshirts painted with cat designs, pet portraits, and even custom-made cat toys and feeding bowls are just a few ideas that crafters can develop and sell. If there is a retail store in your town that specializes in all things feline, visit and acquaint yourself with the merchandise already on the market. Perhaps you have found a potential customer for your kitty wares! *Cat Fancy* magazine caters to serious devotees of pure-bred cats, but it also has many advertisements for merchandise that will give you creative ideas. "Christmas cats" are hot—little kitties with Santa hats and furry faces peeking out of green felt stockings; ornaments and other hanging decorations are snapped up at craft fairs during the holiday season.

The best way to sell this type of merchandise at a weekend craft fair is to offer a wide variety of merchandise at your booth. Instead of a small booth that only offers painted Victorian wooden cats, for instance, why not convince a few other crafters to produce cat-related crafts and sell their wares at your booth as well? You will increase everyone's odds of having a successful fair. Once you establish yourself as a cat-craft entrepreneur you might want to investigate the weekend cat show circuit. Cat shows happen all over the country every weekend and the shows always have booths with high-priced merchandise. This is a much more serious undertaking and more expensive than selling at craft fairs, but if you decide that this is the perfect business for you it is worth checking out.

Chile Wreaths and Other Southwestern Crafts

The heart of the Southwest, Santa Fe, New Mexico, has often been voted one of the favorite travel destinations in the United States by the readers of *Condé Nast Traveler,* and Southwestern-themed crafts continue to travel off the shelves in a big way! To cash in on the mania for Southwestern merchandise here are two different things you can try:

Chile Ristras and Wreaths

Chile ristras are long strings of red or green chile peppers that cooks like to hang in their kitchens for decoration or for a handy ingredient. You can make inexpensive chile ristras yourself by first growing chile peppers (very easy to grow!) and then stringing them together on heavy-duty fishing line. Wreaths are also easy to make with chiles, and very popular items not only at Christmas but year-round. Other interesting chile-related Christmas crafts are miniature trees made from chiles, and long swags of greenery decorated with chiles for accent color.

Coyote Cutouts

The "trickster" Coyote is a potent and popular symbol of the Southwest, and standing wooden coyotes are perennial craft fair favorites. To find a good pattern, flip through Southwestern magazines and design magazines until you find the silhouette of the howling coyote. Enlarge it on a copy machine and *voilà!* you have a pattern to use for wooden cutouts. Coyotes can be window decorations, doorstops, hanging ornaments, and whatever else strikes your fancy. One enterprising weekend entrepreneur markets mailbox flags of the howling coyote! Paint the coyotes in Southwestern desert colors, lots of turquoise, sand, faded pink, and sunset orange.

Quilts, tea cozies and oven mitts with a Southwestern theme are also popular crafts fair items. You might find your needle and thread inspired by this book:

> *Contemporary Southwestern Quilts: A Practical Guide to Developing Original Quilt Designs*
> Mary Evangeline Dillon
> Chilton
> $14.95

Arts and Crafts/Mission Style

Just as Southwestern style began to gain in popularity across the nation in the early 1980s, now the growth is in what is known as Mission style or Arts and Crafts. It is difficult to describe the actual styles, but once you familiarize yourself with it you will see that this style of furniture and decorative objects now fills the pages of *Architectural Digest* magazine and other top home-design magazines.

What kinds of Arts and Crafts or Mission-style products can you make? Just about any wooden product like a napkin holder, a picture frame, or a letter holder can be given this kind of a feel. Learn more by flipping through the glossy style books listed below, or by reading *American Bungalow* magazine to gain an understanding of how to incorporate the design elements.

In addition to wooden objects, crafters are also making pottery in the Arts and Crafts or Mission style, and needle-workers are creating beautiful handmade curtains, pillows, and table linens embroidered with these designs. Once you learn how to imitate this style you will be able to dream up your own crafty ways to incorporate it into hot-selling craft items.

American Bungalow
123 S. Baldwin Ave.
P.O. Box 756
Sierra Madre, CA 91025-0756
(818) 355-1651

American Bungalow Style
Robert Winter and Alexander Vertikoff
Simon and Schuster
$40

In the Arts and Crafts Style
Barbara Mayer
Chronicle Books
$35

Custom Window Coverings with Matching Bedspreads and Quilts

Although she started by sewing "anything," after two years in business Jaydine Rendall has found the perfect way to make extra money—sewing custom window treatments. "My grand-mother taught me to sew; it really is a lost art nowadays. When I decided to stay home with the kids I investigated many different part-time businesses, everything from Avon, to typing, to com-puter stuff. But I decided to turn to what I knew—sewing. I'm able to work six to ten hours a week, and I average about $20 an hour for my time. It's a great home-based business for a mom!"

Jaydine had made her own valances years before, and to brush up on her technique she bought one book on sewing window treatments. She runs an advertisement in the Yellow

Pages under "Window Dressing," and that one ad brings her enough business to stay as busy as she'd like. "January and February are pretty slow months. I get to spend more time with my kids. In the spring there seem to be lots of new baby rooms that need custom curtains, and in the fall everyone goes crazy trying to spruce their house up for the holidays." The demand for curtains for new baby rooms developed into another service that Jaydine offers: custom bedspreads and pillows to match the curtains.

The customers buy the fabric and bring it to Jaydine's home; she then has an in-depth consultation with the customers about what kind of a look they want to achieve. "Not everyone is easy to work with," she warns. "Some people are just never pleased, and if I sense that during our first meeting I will tell them that I can't do the job. I am busy enough that I don't have to take jobs from difficult people. That is one of the benefits of working for yourself: You can choose your clients carefully." During the initial meeting, Jaydine asks for a 50% deposit up front, with full payment due upon completion.

A Southern California woman who has operated several successful sewing businesses has written a book to help other sewing entrepreneurs begin:

> The "Business" of Sewing: How to Start, Maintain, and Achieve Success
> Barbara Wright Sykes
> Collins Publications
> (800) 247-6553
> $14.95

Furniture and Garden Accessories

"Well, I guess you could say my wife got me started. She saw a bench that she liked in an issue of *Country Living* magazine and she kept after me for years to make it. I finally did, and that bench got so many compliments and requests from our friends and neighbors that I started making them for sale." Don Ballard laughed as he described his woodworking SAM to me. "Those benches live on porches all over the country now, and I get a big kick out of that."

For the past three years, Don, a contractor by profession, has been making benches, windmills, whirligigs, and angels in his woodshop at home and selling them to friends and at craft fairs. All of his products have a "country" feel to them. He believes that most people who decorate with the country style are seeking a warmer, more welcome atmosphere, and, "My bench sitting on the front porch surely does look welcome!"

Don makes his wooden benches out of differing grades of pine. The most expensive bench is $180, made from high-grade clear pine, but he sometimes uses less expensive wood to deliver a less expensive finished product. "Most of my benches are sold through word-of-mouth. They are really too expensive to sell at crafts fairs. When I do crafts fairs I try to have as many items under $10 as possible, lots of rubber-band revolvers, small Christmas angels, and toy windmills. At $180 I hardly ever sell the benches."

Unique designs sell the best, he advises. Although his bench was inspired by a picture in a magazine, he modified it quite a bit, shortening the legs so that women's legs will touch the ground and angling the back in order to make it more comfortable to sit in. "That's what people are looking for, the special touch that they can't find at a furniture store."

Woodworkers considering selling their wares should first consider the market. "Check out a bunch of crafts fairs to see what is already out there and how much it costs. And the most important thing to think about," Don warns, "is whether this is how you want to spend all of your free time. I enjoy my woodworking and I spend my spare hours in my woodshop producing things to sell. But not everybody wants to spend their time that way."

A good beginner's book on this topic is:

Building Outdoor Furniture
Percy W. Blanford
Tab Books
$15.95

Don't be intimidated by the idea of woodworking. There are plenty of women around the country who have conquered their fear of high-powered saws and learned to enjoy making furniture and other large crafts with power tools. If you don't have anyone in your life who can teach you how to use this kind of equipment safely (an important first step) ask at your local hardware store and see if they know of any woodworking classes for women. Making furniture can be very lucrative, so don't let your fear of the unknown hold you back!

Hand-Rolled Beeswax Candles

My success as a candlemaker began with an innocent remark from my Auntie Bee. "Oh Jennifer, have I ever taken you to the little candle shop in Carmel?" Auntie Bee (and yes, this is her real name) had discovered a small shop on Ocean Avenue that sold flat sheets of beeswax that can be rolled into several sizes and shapes of candles. One five-minute lesson in rolling candles and I was immediately hooked. For years I made these beeswax candles to give away as gifts at birthdays, Christmas, and housewarmings. But as I began to notice how much these candles sold for in gift shops and through mail-order catalogs, my generous attitude changed. The retail prices were several times what it cost me to make mine and I soon realized that I could easily sell my hand-rolled candles and undercut the prices. A weekend business was born!

I buy the flat sheets of colored beeswax from several sources, depending on which colors they stock. Not all of the suppliers carry all of the colors, and throughout the year my customers' whims change. Red and green sell well at Christmas, brown, dark wine, and other warm colors sell during Thanksgiving, and pastels sell well in summer. I offer three different sizes: 6-inch tapers, 12-inch tapers, and a thick and handsome, long-burning 6-inch centerpiece candle. Each candle takes only 30 seconds or so to produce, an evening spent rolling candles while watching television can produce enough candles to last throughout a typical afternoon craft fair. My wholesale cost for the wax sheets and the wicks (the only two elements required) averages around $1. From each sheet I can either produce two 8-inch-high tapers, or one long 16-inch taper. My retail prices for hand-rolled beeswax candles are:

two 6-inch tapers $4.50	(actual cost, $1; profit, $3.50)
two 12-inch tapers $8	(actual cost, $2; profit, $6)
four 6-inch tapers $8	(actual cost, $2; profit $6)
one 6-inch, long-burning centerpiece candle $10	(actual cost, $2; profit $8)

My husband, Peter, is a dedicated woodworker, and he has added to my wares by producing redwood candleholders from recycled redwood and leftover odds and ends from other projects. I sell short, thick candles in redwood candleholders, decorated with a small seasonal wreath or an elegant silk ribbon bow, for $12. The finished candles are sold primarily at local craft fairs and holiday bazaars, but I also do a brisk business among my co-workers at Christmas time. To give you a sense of what a typical afternoon of sales is like, here is a quick report on sales at my booth at the Granite Bay Christian Preschool First Annual Crafts Fair in the month of November:

I arrived at 8 A.M., per the little instruction sheet that I had been mailed. My booth space was just inside the doorway in a converted kindergarten room. Dragging my folding teak table from the back of the car, I began to build my candle display. I have a rather elaborate look that I try to duplicate every time that I sell at a craft fair; my theory is to try to make potential customers want my products because they want to achieve the "lifestyle" that I portray. To achieve that end I create a tabletop display to rival any Bloomingdale's Christmas window—gleaming antique silver candlesticks, soft linen tablecloth, carefully arranged beeswax candles tied in pairs with gold silk ribbons, cut crystal bowls filled with dried flowers (also for sale, foraged of course!). I have a large standing screen covered with rich-looking fabric to place behind the table and direct the eye towards my beautiful wares. Can't leave anything to chance. . . .

My space at the craft fair cost $30, so I would not begin to make my goal of $100 until I passed my first $30. Open to the public at ten o'clock, I edged above break-even by 11:30. Throughout the day I had steady sales, but I also lost many others due to an oversight on my part—I had failed to anticipate that Christmas colors would be in demand before Thanksgiving. If only I had brought another dozen pair of red candles!! My total take for the day was $119, working from 8:00 A.M. until the fair closed at 4:00 P.M. Not the best ever, but it gave me a clue to what customers would be looking for the following weekend at a larger fair. I packed my car with my display and my unsold candles and headed straight for the beekeeping supply store to buy as many sheets of red beeswax as I could!

Not content to tell only about my own candle-selling experiences, I contacted another successful beeswax candle crafter to see what kind of advice she had for weekend entrepreneurs: "I have been selling handmade beeswax candles every other weekend at the Jack London Square Farmers' Market in Oakland for years," Pat Hill told me. "I used to offer both the basic cylinder type as well as the fancy spiral type, but since the spirals outsold the other by two to one I dropped that choice. I sell my spiral candles for $2 a pair and, combined with selling jars of our homegrown honey, I make anywhere between $300 to $600 a day. It is definitely worth my time!"

Learning how to make beeswax candles is not difficult. Check the class schedule at your local crafts store. Beekeeping supply stores are another good source. I have been able to purchase a broad range of materials at a beekeeping store in Sacramento, California. Once you find a source for the flat sheets of wax, check their prices and keep digging for other sources. Prices range from $1.90 per sheet to $1 per sheet, and the lowest price I have seen is 69¢ per sheet! The lower your cost for goods, the greater your profit on your products, so always be on the lookout for better sources. If you are unable to find a store in your area that carries beeswax sheets, here are mail-order sources:

Sacramento Beekeeping Supplies (916) 451-2337
The Honey Comb (916) 773-1693
B&B Honey Farm (507) 896-3955
Candlewick Company (215) 348-9285
The A.I. Root Company (800) BUY-ROOT

Scented Wax Candles and Gifts

I am already planning to add another product to my craft fair offering next Christmas—scented beeswax and paraffin Christmas tree ornaments. By adding scents like musk, vanilla, lavender, or other scents to the warm, melted wax and then pouring it into molds to harden, you can make beautiful gift items to sell. The molds come in animal shapes, angel shapes, and also intricate candle molds. Nancy Stewart, the owner of Sacramento Beekeeping Supplies (they carry the supplies for scented wax candles), told me about a customer who was doing so well at farmers' markets with scented wax gifts that she had quit her full-time job!

I found inspiration (and instructions) for scented ornaments in the following book:

Gifts from the Herb Garden
Emelie Tolley and Chris Mead
Clarkson Potter
$20

As you can see, despite the fact that the hot selling season is only early October until just before Christmas, thinking about craft fairs is a year-round preoccupation! The greater the selection and the more varied the merchandise, the better the chance that your sales will soar.

Soap Making

One more idea on how to make money from bees is soap. Although handmade soap has sort of a '70s back-to-nature or *Dr.*

Quinn, Medicine Woman sound to it, handmade soaps still make for popular items at farmers' markets and craft fairs. The fastest-selling soaps seem to be those that are also beautifully wrapped in handmade paper and tied with raffia string or a lovely ribbon. As with other types of handmade crafts, presentation and packaging go a long way toward helping your customers decide that they just can't live without what you have made.

The Art of Soap Making
Merilyn Mohr
Firefly
$9.95

Soaps, Shampoos & Other Luxuries
Kelly Reno
Prima Publishing
$12

The wonderful folks at Sacramento Beekeeping Supplies also carry soap-making supplies. See their listing under *Hand-Rolled Beeswax Candles.*

Patterns for Tole Painters

Tole painting is a popular craft, and Lisa Soderborg of Denver, Colorado, has found a terrific extra-income opportunity as a result of her interest in tole painting. "Tole painters are always looking for interesting wood patterns on which to paint, and I started making my own six years ago. Once my fellow tole painters found out that I could cut patterns, they started to come to me with pattern books asking me to make this shape or that shape. I didn't really sit down and plan this business, it just sort of happened!"

Lisa buys pine lumber in all different sizes, and custom-cuts it for her customers. As a full-time mom with another one on the way, she finds that her pattern-cutting business can easily be run in her spare time. "I go out to my shop and cut when the kids are in bed, or in school, whenever I have some extra time. It's a great stress-reliever for a mother." Over the years Lisa has acquired more equipment. After starting out with just a scroll saw, she now owns a bandsaw, router, belt sander, drill press, palm sander, and a jigsaw. Not very glamorous, she says, but good solid equipment that she feels confident and comfortable using.

To set prices for custom pattern cutting Lisa makes sure she is making at least $10 an hour for her time, and also passes the full cost of the wood along to the customer. Her busiest seasons are October through December, with a flurry of activity around Easter. Lisa limits her work to custom pattern cutting on demand, but encourages other woodworkers to approach craft and hobby supply stores about carrying custom-designed patterns for tole painters. Do research at the stores and among crafters to learn what types of patterns are the most popular before creating your product.

Picture Frames

There are wonderful ways to decorate picture frames in such a way that the finished product flies off your table at a craft fair. Check for inexpensive finished frames at garage and rummage sales, the 98-cent Clearance Centers, thrift stores, and anywhere else you can find cheap frames to start with, then decorate them in any of several ways:

- Dried flowers—Hot-glue dried moss, herbs, and flowers around the frame to give it a country garden feel. Check out the section on *Foraging the Wild for Profit* in Chapter 3 for ideas on how and where to find natural materials for free.

- Decoupage—For my own decoupage projects I like to use pictures and artwork from fancy magazines. In a hand-crafted goods store in Boulder, Colorado, I once saw a mirror in a frame that was decoupaged with cut-up pictures of oriental rugs, all put together in a mosaic fashion. Something you or I could have created in two hours, and the price was $150! If you have a good eye for cleverly arranging things, try this on a frame.

- Old maps—Buy old books of maps or loose maps at garage sales and wrap the edges of the frames, then finish with a decoupage mixture. Frames decorated with maps have a well-traveled air about them and are popular with folks who want to frame their travel photos in an unusual manner.

To set prices for your frames, don't forget to factor in the cost of the frame along with your time and other materials. Consult this book for more ideas:

Making & Decorating Picture Frames
Janet Bridge
North Light Books
$24.99

Porcelain Dolls and Christmas Ceramics

While working full-time for the State of California, Cindy Davis has a flourishing part-time business creating porcelain dolls and custom ceramics. "I learned how to paint and fire the dolls from a woman in town who owned a doll shop. Once I felt confident enough to work on my own I bought a kiln and took it from there. Most towns have porcelain doll shops and ceramics stores; look in the Yellow Pages under 'dolls' or 'ceramics' in order to find one where you can take lessons." Cindy works on her own at home to produce her wares, but buys the basic unfired materials from the shops.

Her dolls are works of art. Cindy paints each one individually and hand-sews the clothing. Sold mostly through word-of-mouth, the dolls go for as much as $300. "Each one has its own personality; sometimes it is hard to sell them after I have worked on them so long. They are like my little babies!"

Ceramic Christmas trees are easier to part with. Cindy buys the greenware from the ceramics shop and hand-paints each tree before firing it in the kiln. She does a brisk business in the pre-holiday craft fair season with her trees, selling the 16-inch model for as much as $60 and the smaller versions for $30 to $50. The more expensive trees include music boxes and blinking lights to add to the price. "I make a greater profit on the dolls than I do on the Christmas trees," Cindy admits. "But they sell much faster at the crafts fairs than the dolls do. The wholesale price on the undecorated trees is around $38. I make a $20 profit by the time I decorate and sell it."

Painted Ukranian Eggs

Two years ago Amy Clark hatched her own business painting Ukranian-style eggs which retail anywhere from $12 to $175. After painting the eggs as a hobby for years she worked up the courage to display her wares at the Davis, California, Farmers' Market. In her first two days she earned $600, and she hasn't stopped since.

Her sales during her busiest seasons, Christmas and Easter, now approach $6,000. Not bad for a woman who once thought to herself, "Who would pay $15 for a painted egg?"

Painted eggs (*pysanky*) are an art form that originated in Central Europe. Similar to the tie-dying we learned in the '70s, the technique involves using beeswax to draw a design on a plain white egg, which is then dipped into dye. A coat of varnish goes on the finished egg, innards and all. The egg and yolk eventually dry out.

To learn more about how to paint eggs, check this book out of the library or find it at your local booksellers:

> *Decorating Eggs: Exquisite Designs with Wax and Dye*
> Jane Pollack
> Sterling/Lark
> $24.95

Handmade Greeting Cards

Not everyone is pleased to receive a Hallmark card. Some folks prefer buying and receiving unusual or one-of-a-kind greeting cards that have a slightly more personal feel to them. Greeting cards are popular items at craft shows and at retail stores that specialize in handmade items. And small extra-income entrepreneurs like Paper Pearls in Citrus Heights, California, fill a real need for the consumer. By combining handmade papers purchased at an art supply store with lace and ribbon purchased at a fabric store, along with thin twigs she fashions into hearts and glues into place, this enterprising woman makes lovely little cards to sell on the weekends.

For more ideas on how to create handmade greeting cards:

Card Crafting: Over 45 Ideas for Making Greeting Cards and Stationery
Gillian Souter
Sterling
$12.95

Potpourri and Herbal Products

Working as a nurse and a respiratory therapist in Anacortes, Washington, Darcy Tietjen has seen enough of what chemicals can do to our bodies. She started her own part-time potpourri and herbal products company, Proverbs 31 Woman, so that she could work with and sell all-natural products. "We moved into a new house that had 24 beautiful rose plants already well-established in the garden. I thought it would be such a waste to just throw the flowers away when they were through blooming. I bought a book to learn how to make potpourri and rose waters, and I was on my way!"

Darcy now has an extensive product line and sells her wares at craft fairs and in local crafters' galleries and boutiques. Her full line includes expensive items like rose waters and bath vinegars bottled in antique glass bottles, and always includes lower-priced items to attract impulse gift shoppers. Small handmade soaps are priced under $1 and are meant to be used as stocking-stuffers or as an attractive topping for a wrapped package. She recommends that other crafters follow this same pricing philosophy. After two years in business, Darcy is choosy about which craft fairs she attends and who is putting them on. "It matters to me who the organizer is," she says. "The organizer and the kind of advertising and coverage they choose makes a big difference in who attends. I really like church bazaars." Craft shows take a lot of time on the weekends, Darcy warns, Friday and Saturday are the two biggest days. Craft boutiques and galleries are another outlet for her wares; she leaves them on consignment in several places throughout the county.

"This is not a business for dilettantes; if you are easily bored and start up many projects at once then this is not a business for you." She advises prospective potpourri makers and sellers to look long and hard at the future—if you really want to devote the time and effort it will take to succeed, go for it. "It takes awhile to get established. There are real ups and downs, but it is worth it!"

In addition to Darcy's success, I'd like to share a business idea that I created several years ago for a cousin. His parents live in Carmel, and were more than a bit annoyed that their just-graduated-from-college son was spending most the summer hanging around the house doing nothing. "Hmmm . . . Carmel? Quaint little beach town with a steady supply of tourists? Do I have an idea for you!" I said, and here is what I suggested:

Potpourri is big business, and in any quaint tourist town there is the potential to capitalize on this craze for scents. Forage for materials that are common to the area (in Carmel, for instance, I recommended eucalyptus leaves and seedpods, pine needles, and small sea shells) to use as bulk in the potpourri, then add the scent. You will have a product that will appeal to tourists who would like to take home a small, inexpensive souvenir, as well as a product that gift stores will be happy to stock. Design a nice package and you are on your way! "Carmel Essence" was easily created from foraged materials, but it could just as easily be "Tahoe Pines," "Oregon Forest," or "Carolina Coast." Help yourself to my idea, and let me know how it works. My cousin never did follow up; he became a stockbroker instead.

How to get started making potpourris and other herbal products? There are several good books on the market, filled with recipes, drying tips, and instructions. They are primarily available in hardcover. "Books are probably my single biggest business expense," says Darcy. "Whenever I see a new one published I just have to pick it up and see if there is any new information I need." Before you decide to take the plunge into this type of a SAM, you might want to see if your local library has books on this topic. Once you are committed, look for these books in your local bookstore:

> *The Scented Room: Cherchez's Book of Dried Flowers, Fragrance, and Potpourri*
> Barbara Milo Ohrbach
> Clarkson N. Potter
> $15.95

> *The Complete Book of Nature Crafts: How to Make Wreaths, Dried Flower Arrangements, Potpourris, Dolls, Baskets, Gifts, Decorative Accessories for the Home, and Much More*
> Eric Carlson, Dawn Cusick, and Carol Taylor
> Rodale Press
> $27.95

Finding wholesale suppliers is always difficult when starting any type of business. Many crafting magazines carry ads for potpourri suppliers, and here are a few:

> San Francisco Herb Company
> (415) 861-3018 or (800) 227-4530

> The Essential Oil Company
> Free catalog: (800) 729-5912
> In Oregon, (503) 697-5992

> Frontier Cooperative Herbs
> Box 299
> Norway, IA 52318
> (319) 227-7996

To learn more about fast-selling homemade products like herbal vinegars and herbal oils, here are two books that I recommend:

> *Gifts from the Herb Garden*
> Emelie Tolley and Chris Mead
> Clarkson Potter
> $20

> *The Herbal Pantry*
> Emelie Tolley and Chris Mead
> Clarkson Potter
> $20

Thinking It Through

America has gone crazy for crafts, and fairs and boutiques to fuel this passion have sprung up across the country. Crafters of all description are successfully displaying and selling their wares at these shows, but there are also crafters who sit alone and unappreciated at their booths because their wares are not quite up to snuff. Before you gear up to produce your crafts on a large scale, take the time to give your product a critical look. Is it well made? Useful? Affordable? Unique? Ask your friends for an honest evaluation of your wares and pay attention to their suggestions. Don't be hurt if you fail to pass their scrutiny; consider how much time and effort you have just saved yourself! Back to the drawing board for another idea. . . .

Most cities and towns have crafting classes available through a craft store, the local Parks and Recreation Department, or private instruction. Take advantage of the knowledge available in classes and, who knows, perhaps once you master a craft and achieve success at the fairs you can add to your profits by offering instruction!

Almost every crafter I spoke to returned again and again to the topic of pricing. Pricing your wares is a critical element for success: It is better to sell large quantities of low-priced items than to sell nothing at all because your products are too expensive. Try to detach your ego from the price tag.

Profit is an important element of success, and sometimes crafters have a difficult time approaching it in a businesslike manner. Because so many crafters started as hobbyists, it is sometimes difficult to develop a more professional attitude toward it as an extra-income opportunity. Always try to make at least twice as much as you have paid for your supplies.

Like any other business where your ego is on the line, be prepared to handle rejection. Many shoppers will walk by your booth, glance down at your beautiful handmade wares, and keep on walking. This can be difficult to take, but if you have first tested the quality of your products among friends and relatives, you can reassure yourself that what you are offering simply doesn't fit that person's need.

Do not feel embarrassed and rejected every time someone fails to buy. Focus on the wonderful feeling you get when someone loves your products, buys out everything you have made, and then displays it in his or her home.

To keep your products current with popular trends, it is important to read the crafting magazines on the market. Not only will you learn what is hot and new, but you will run across new ideas (along with instructions!) for more crafts to sell. Among the most popular crafting magazines available on newsstands is *Crafts 'n Things.* Once you decide to approach your hobby with a more businesslike attitude it is a good idea to subscribe to *The Crafts Report.* This monthly tabloid is filled with interesting articles about professional crafters, lists complete state-by-state information on upcoming craft fairs, and is a good source for leads on wholesale suppliers. A one-year subscription is $29; call (800) 777-7098.

Let me share another major source of inspiration and ideas with you—Martha Stewart. Watch her television show, read her magazine, *Martha Stewart Living,* and you will notice how much of what she does can easily be done on a larger scale and sold at craft fairs. Beautiful and inspired designs for up-to-the minute, fashionable ideas—what more can you ask for? Some people like to laugh at her, but I say "Thanks, Martha, what a great idea!" Besides, you can write off your subscription to her magazine as a business expense!

Chapter Five

Odds and Ends—
Great SAMs That
Defy Categories

Some things in life don't fit neatly into categories, and the entrepreneurs in this chapter sure don't either! Here are some wacky ideas, some silly ideas, and some downright strange ideas, but rest assured they are all terrific Sources of Additional Money. If you have the talent, the skills, or live in the sort of special area where some of these business ideas will work, get started immediately on these creative ways to make extra cash.

Designing and Leading Custom Tours

Bruce Kayton has an unusual knowledge about a seldom-seen side of New York City's districts and neighborhoods—he knows the history of "radical New York." For $6 he will lead you on a 2.5-hour tour unlike any you have ever experienced, pointing out where Emma Goldman lived and Abbie Hoffman hid. In the past two years he has led over a thousand people on walking tours of New York.

In San Francisco, Shirley Fong-Torres takes groups of up to 12 on gourmet food and shopping tours of the world-famous

Chinatown area, stopping to watch noodle factories at work and to partake of Chinese delicacies.

In Sacramento, Randy Gudelka leads history buffs on walking tours of that city's colorful past. All of these quirky tour leaders base their success on a genuine interest and personal knowledge of their subjects, and are fortunate to live in large cities rife with color, culture, and history. But you don't have to live in a big city to create and lead unusual tours. With a little imagination and a lot of research you can come up with your own tour idea that will work in your area.

Leading unique tours is a perfect SAM for a part-time entrepreneur—weekends are ideal for this kind of tour. Most walking tours should last between two and three hours, and tour prices range from $5 to $10. Bruce Kayton sometimes draws 50 people for his Radical Tours, not a bad way to earn $300 in an afternoon.

There are endless possibilities for tour ideas. Live out in the country? Why not develop a guided tour of "U-Pick-It" farms and lead a group of food-loving city folk from farm to farm, berry picking and pea plucking, ending up in a great down-home restaurant. During the fall you could organize a driving tour of beautiful autumn leaves and colors. The countryside has history, too. Research the major events that have taken place over the years and develop an exciting and informative talk. This is not a pursuit for shy people; to succeed as a tour leader you must feel comfortable talking in front of groups. A sense of humor doesn't hurt either.

To get started in designing a specialized tour of your area, here are the best general topics. Study them and be creative about the special "twists" that you could give them in your town or area:

1. Food—Is your region known for a particular specialty food or regional cuisine? Is fresh produce grown nearby or unique products manufactured? Are there brew-pubs or small wineries in the area?

2. History— Literary history, battle sights, and even scandal have all been the basis for successful tours. In Los Angeles and in Paris, tours are given of "permanent residents," those famous folks who are found in graveyards!

3. Scenery—Autumn leaves, unknown waterfalls, wildlife, bird-watching, and acres of flowering tulips are popular starting points.

4. Art—Outdoor sculpture, architectural details, even unusual neon signs could work.

Look around your city or region with a new perspective. What is unusual there, which might be of interest to others? What about your own knowledge and interests? What topic do you know about that would interest a group of strangers willing to pay $5 each to learn? Knowledge of your topic is the key to success in developing an unusual tour and gaining a following. Shirley Fong-Torres of Wok Wiz advises, "The top-of-the-list requirement for success is to have great knowledge of your topic. You must have a love for the topic; the public can see right through you if you don't. I have a true love for the food and the history of Chinatown." Once you find a quirky idea that you think will work, become an expert and learn all that you can. Practice giving your tour to friends and family before you try to attract paying customers.

When you have developed your expertise, designed a tour, and feel comfortable with your topic, you are ready to begin leading tours. Write a press release and send it out to the media. If your tour is unusual enough they will cover it. Free media coverage is always worth trying and can be a big boost. Many small newspapers have "events" sections where you can list your tour. Once you have used up all avenues for free coverage, place small ads in newspapers and magazines that would interest the type of folks you are trying to attract. Shirley Fong-Torres advertises Wok Wiz in the regional magazines certain to be read by the foodies who might take her tour. Advertise historic tours in the local museum newsletter, and try to reach art lovers through galleries. Be creative about reaching your audience; once you have established a following, your satisfied tourists will begin to do your advertising for you! Tourists and locals alike will be interested in what you have to offer. A woman in San Francisco advertises her Walk Tours "for anyone who wants to be a San Franciscan for a day—or for old-time San Franciscans who just want to know more about their city."

To learn more about how to develop and run your own small custom tour business, take a look at the following useful book. Although much of the content is geared toward a large-scale operation, you will be able to pick up quite a bit of helpful information.

Start and Run a Profitable Tour Guiding Business
Barbara Braidwood, Susan M. Boyce, and Richard Cropp
Self-Counsel Press
$14.95

Environmental and "New Age" Products

Our world is changing around us, and concern for the environment is becoming more and more mainstream. We are becoming more spiritually aware. These two movements, the environmental movement, and the New Age movement, have spawned many a successful extra income.

"For years I marveled at the way my wife's family exchanged their gifts. They have so many kids that every year at Christmas there are likely to be upwards of 200 gifts under the tree. But after the gifts were exchanged there was no huge mountain of ripped wrapping paper and ribbon to throw away. As thrifty home-sewers they had devised a simple cloth and ribbon gift bag that could be used year after year. I was so impressed by this method that I wanted to introduce the whole world to the idea." And that is how full-time natural foods wholesaler Francis Hamilton of Grass Valley, California, founded his spare-time company, Baggits.

Baggits makes one thing and one thing only: cloth bags in different sizes and materials, designed to be used to wrap gifts or hold scented sachets and potpourris. Early on, Francis decided not to sell directly to the public, but to rely on small retailers throughout Northern California. "I guarantee each retailer that carries Baggits an exclusive in their area. It's not fair to a small store if I offer my product all over town. Why should they carry it if their neighbor does too?" Many of his local accounts are consignment accounts which Francis services himself. His largest single account, however, is a mail-order catalog that specializes in environmentally friendly products.

The future is bright for environmentally friendly goods and services. "When the full cost of disposal is reflected in the cost of the product to the consumer, then a lot more manufacturers will become environmentally friendly," Francis predicts. "Any product, any way of doing anything out there, can be done in a way that is better for the planet. I'd encourage anyone to try to develop a product like this. We'll all be better off in the long run!"

There are pitfalls to manufacturing and selling a product on a part-time basis, however. Baggits has grown as large as it can with the time and money that Francis can devote to it. "If my orders increased tremendously at this point, so would my capital demands. People should understand that production requires a fair amount of money up front and that increased success also means increased investment of time and money. Know what it is that you want to achieve, and make sure that you have enough time left in the day to do it!" Keep your eyes open for ways in which the things already around us could be made better and you will take the first step toward developing an environmentally friendly product.

Have you stepped inside a New Age store lately? Many of the items that are sold in stores, through catalogs, and at outdoor fairs are made by New Age weekend entrepreneurs. Crystal wands, Indian drums, sage smudges, and similar items are hand-crafted at home to meet the growing demand. "Herb-filled 'dream pillows' are the fastest-selling product that we have right now," says the manager of Native Scents in Taos, New Mexico. Herbal dream pillows are filled with lavender, mugwort, rose petals, white sage, hops, yerba santa, and other assorted herbs, and when placed under your regular pillow is supposed to encourage deep sleep. Hand-rolled and tied sage smudge bundles are used increasingly by alternative doctors, therapists, and body workers to purify the air and to attract positive and beneficial energies.

Maggie Lee of Terra Flora has a part-time business catering to the growing interest in New Age products. Her company produces and sells a package of mixed herbs designed for herbal steam baths and sweat lodges. She packages her herbs in biodegradable cellophane and ties them with hand-dyed, desert-toned raffia. Small instruction cards printed on recycled card stock are tucked under the raffia tie. Maggie's products sell well in the Southwest and she is working to expand her market across the country and into New Age stores in other states.

Another big trend in the New Age market is an interest in angels. Yes, that's right, those guys and girls with halos and wings. Books about angels, greeting cards, art, dolls, anything with an angelic theme is moving off the shelf. Look around at what the market already offers and see if there is an angel-related product missing. Maybe you are just the weekend entrepreneur to make it soar!

Gift Baskets

Who had ever heard of a gift basket until the last few years? Suddenly they are everywhere, under every Christmas tree and on the doorstep of every new real estate client. This is a competitive field, but if you can come up with unique ideas and products and offer your customers an unusual twist there is still room for part-time gift basket entrepreneurs.

In Auburn, California, Christie McKinnon runs her part-time gift basket business, Bodacious Basket Company, as a sideline to her cruise-only tour company. "With the tour business my income tends to fluctuate greatly from month to month, so I look to the gift baskets to even that out." Christie got started by taking a class at the local Learning Exchange, "How to Make Gift Baskets for Profit." Following her teacher's advice she makes specialty baskets for all occasions—baby showers, New Year's, anniversaries, birthdays, weddings, romantic occasions, and using her travel background wisely, a "vacation in a basket." The vacation in a basket is generally ordered by one spouse to surprise another and includes champagne, airline or cruise tickets, and other travel goodies like suntan lotion, sunglasses, and wacky shorts. Christie's price range for her gift baskets is $20 to $200. Lower-priced baskets sell faster, but for very special occasions the sky seems to be the limit, especially when airline tickets are added in!

Start-up costs are relatively low in the gift basket business, and Christie found a great way to lower them even further. "Instead of buying a hand-held shrink wrap machine for $400 I went to my local hardware store and bought one of those heat-gun paint peelers. Works great!" You must have a wholesale license to buy products for your baskets. Gourmet food products are popular right now and so are personal care products. Whatever the contents, gift baskets seem to be a welcome treat for the recipient and are growing in popularity.

To decide the price of your gift basket, use the following formula: Add up the wholesale cost of everything in the basket (don't forget to add the cost of the basket itself) and triple it. That will give you the retail price to charge and ensure a tidy profit. For instance, if the wholesale value of the contents of a basket, plus the basket, is $15, retail that basket for $45. A quick $30 profit for you!

How many different types of gift baskets are there? Hundreds! What about a "bath basket" with bubble bath, body oil, sponges, and talcum powder? Or a "gourmet chef" basket filled with spices, wire whisks, recipe cards, and a cookbook? "Afternoon tea" is a great idea, filled with exotic teas, delicate china cups, and linen napkins. What about a "classic cinema" basket filled with a few old black-and-white films on video, some popcorn, and a box of Good 'N' Plenty candy! Once you start creating a few gift baskets the ideas will begin to flow.

Gift baskets can be marketed several ways. Christie put the word on her wares out among friends who work in large state office buildings and started to get customers right away. Some creative marketers in Michigan started promoting their gift baskets through home parties styled like Tupperware parties. Linking up with real estate agents, insurance agents, large corporations, or anyone who regularly sends gifts to clients is a terrific source of steady business.

The gift basket industry has grown up in the last few years and now has an industry magazine and an annual trade show. The magazine, *Gift Basket Review*, is filled with inspirational stories about successful gift basket marketers, as well as advertisements for wholesale suppliers who cater to the gift basket industry.

Gift Basket Idea Newsletter
(303) 575-5676
$5/issue

Gift Basket Review
Festivities Publications
$29.95/year

Building a Better Gift Basket Business
Festivities Publications
$49.95

The Gift Basket Video Series
Festivities Publications
$39.95 each

Festivities Publications
815 Haines St.
Jacksonville, FL 32206
(800) 729-6338

Here are some wholesale basket sources:

Willow Specialties
The Rochester Basket Company
(800) 724-7300, (716) 344-2900

Palecek Picnic Baskets
(800) 274-7730

Remember, you must first have a wholesale license before you can order from these basket companies. Contact your State Board of Equalization for more information.

Gift basket businesses are frequently touted as one of the hottest growing businesses in the '90s. That means increased competition. Before you begin a part-time gift basket business first check to see if there is competition in your area. If there are gift basket businesses already, decide if you can offer something different. If you can, go for it!

Holistic Housecleaning

Wanda Adelsberger has a successful Wisconsin-based part-time cleaning business with a twist—she only uses natural products. No chemicals, just homemade products that are gentle on the environment. "It's the times. Anyone with any awareness of what is happening to our planet would consider using this kind of a housecleaning service. I know people all over the country who are doing this and making it work." Wanda finds it to be a great way to make extra money to fund her daughter's interest in gymnastics.

Her prices are comparable to what other housecleaners are charging in her area. "Why charge more just because I use natural products? I want to encourage as many people as possible to live this way, not discourage them by making it costlier. It makes me angry that 'natural food' costs more than junk food. I don't want to make the same mistake in my own business."

Instead of the chemical-laden commercial cleaning products available in grocery stores, Wanda's supplies are much simpler—a mixture of vinegar and water for surface cleaning, and baking soda to use as a scrub. These two products form the basis for all of her cleaning. "Baking soda is a terrific substitute for abrasive scrubs like Comet. Wet the surface, shake it on, let it sit for 10 minutes, and then clean it off. Works great, try it!" She also uses biodegradable Shaklee products, and feels that there are many high-quality natural cleaning products available at health food stores. "Most people use too much stuff on their wood furniture. They just smother it with oils and waxes. Wood needs moisture, but a cloth barely dampened with water works fine to get the dust off and replenish the need for moisture. That business of needing to wax and polish your furniture every week is just an old wives' tale."

One of the best things about offering a holistic housecleaning service is how soon you can get started. "I built this business up from no clients to seven clients within weeks," Wanda says. "The word-of-mouth just spreads like wildfire. A lot of people have just been waiting for something like this to come along."

To succeed in this as a part-time business, be confident about your skills and meticulous about details. "It is the little touches that are important, on top of fan blades, insides and tops of window ledges and blinds, dusting off light bulbs. Having someone else clean your house is a luxury and in order to justify it they must do a better job than the homeowner can do on their own. People will always apply stricter standards to a hired housecleaner's work than they would to their own so be very thorough," Wanda recommends.

In Chicago, Heather's Holistic Housecleaning is cleaning up on a part-time basis, $45 every time she cleans a medium-size house. "This is an absolutely perfect way to make extra money," Heather raves. "And not only can you make extra money, but the work is so physical that I've lost a lot of weight, too!" Heather became a holistic housecleaner when she began reading the labels on cleaning products and noticing how many of them contained pollutants. Most abrasive scrubs, for instance, contain chlorine bleaching agents that create dioxin when they break down. Before starting a cleaning service like Wanda's or Heather's, spend a bit of time reading the labels of standard cleaning products to acquaint yourself with the types of chemicals that you should avoid. Read environmental magazines like those from the Sierra Club to develop a greater awareness of the issues. Your clients will expect you to have a fairly well-developed knowledge of the subject.

Prop Rental

Do you live in a house filled with Victorian antiques? Mimi Luebbermann does, and not long ago she realized that her furniture and knickknacks could provide her with a terrific second income. A full-time writer, Mimi now has an extra income renting out her Victorian things to photographers who need props for the background of shots. To get started with prop rentals she took color pictures of all of her Victorian things, put together a photo album book, and began showing it to art directors at advertising agencies and photographers. The standard rental fee for week-long use of a prop is between 10% to 20%

of the replacement value, so a silver teaspoon that cost $20 to replace would rent for $2. An entire set of silverware that is worth $1,500 would rent for $150. Mimi has valuable words of caution, however, about how important it is to have pictures and documentation on everything that you rent out: "There are a few things out there that I don't think I will ever get back, simply because they were not well documented. It is very important to have a picture of every single piece that has been rented out, and that each of these pieces has been assigned a number. At any given time, then, I can just check my files and see that the Georgian silver serving spoon has not been returned and that it is time to bug the photographer! Develop a system to track your things down to the teeniest item."

Mimi specializes in supplying Victorian props for food photography, and reports a big demand for all different types of silverware, interesting china platters and plates, lacy linens, and unusual serving pieces. Art Deco is also popular among food photographers.

Photographers don't need just Victorian or Art Deco props either. There is a large need for all kinds of things from all kinds of eras. After learning about Mimi's SAM I started to look around at my own possessions with a different eye and realized that I had a big enough collection of travel-related stuff from the '20s that I could easily put together a portfolio to show to photographers. Who wouldn't want one of my well-worn leather suitcases covered with vintage hotel stickers? And wouldn't my ostrich skin jewelry box look fantastic in a high-gloss diamond advertisement? I also own a large collection of old travel postcards—what great background material for an ad! Mimi's success has inspired me to give this business a try, and if you have a great collection of things you should try it!

Not everything will be of interest to photographers. I'm afraid that a collection of old gym socks won't quite cut it, but certainly a collection of old sports equipment would! Having a broad-based collection of things will increase the attractiveness of your collection to potential renters. Mimi recommends having at least 25 different items pictured in your promotional material. I was able to come up with the following 1920s-era collectibles to include in my "Classic Travel Era" prop offering:

Several old leather suitcases (many with hotel and early plane stickers on the sides), an ostrich-skin jewelry case, an original Chanel chantilly lace dress circa 1926, a large selection of old travel postcards, four antique oriental rugs, a polo trophy from a tournament in the South of France, assorted sterling silver pieces (including a classic '20s martini shaker), many old family travel photos showing travelers in classic clothes posed in front of familiar monuments around the world, assorted tourist souvenirs from the era, a small art deco lamp, vintage train schedules and maps, antique cameras, old travel books, Rookwood pottery pieces, vintage U.S. passports, and a dozen women's hats of all descriptions.

I spoke to advertising art director Brian Burch of the Burch Design Group about the business of prop rental: "We pass the cost of prop rental on to the client as a part of the total cost of a project. The right props can sometimes make all the difference in a photo, turning an interesting photograph into a spectacular one. If I received a brochure from someone with a unique collection to rent out and I thought that I might use it someday I would certainly file that information away. Approaching photographers directly is also a good method for people getting into the prop rental business. You can buy lists of professional photographers from the professional organizations that they belong to, and you can also find them in stock workbooks. Anyone with a truly unique collection should be able to make prop renting work."

House Staging

As a variation on prop rental, Mimi also recommends renting large pieces of furniture to realtors who need to furnish a high-priced empty house on the market. In the real estate business this is called "house staging."

Sometimes the owners have had to move to their new location, taking their furniture and leaving a stark empty house behind. Furnished houses sell faster, so real estate agents will rent furniture to create ambiance. One realtor in the Oakland

Hills actually asked the house-stagers to stay for the afternoon and bake cookies in the kitchen to create a warm, inviting atmosphere!

There is an old tale from the early days of the movie business that illustrates the beauty of renting something as a way of making money. One of the Warner brothers saw a film for the first time, noticed how many people had paid a nickel to watch it, and then marveled that afterwards the theater owner still had the film and could show it over and over again. He decided right then and there to get into the movie business. What a great idea to make money from something that you will still own later!

Personal Trainer

Chris Dominguez has been working in his spare time as a personal trainer for 12 years, making $30 an hour for his services. "If I lived in a larger metropolitan area like San Francisco or New York I could charge anywhere from $50 to $100, but in this small town I am happy with $30," he says. Personal trainers design workouts for their clients, help them through the routine, and generally keep them on track with their fitness goals. "Since they pay me up front I give them a reason to show up at the gym! Who's going to blow off their workout if they know it means $30 down the drain?"

Work as a personal trainer is a terrific way to go for aerobics instructors, athletes, dance students, or college students studying exercise physiology, nutrition, anatomy, or kinesiology. "If you are willing to go out and obtain the knowledge, then this is a great part-time business," Chris advises. The most in-demand times for working out with a personal trainer are early in the morning before work, or just after work. You could easily fit your clients in around a full-time or part-time job elsewhere. Personal trainers are popular with executives and professionals because they have limited time to exercise and cannot afford to be injured.

Once you have the knowledge and expertise, it is wise to seek certification from the International Dance and Exercise

Association, the American College of Sports Medicine, the National Strength and Conditioning Association, or the American Council on Exercise. The American Council on Sports Exercise in San Diego, California, offers specialized training for budding personal trainers. Although personal fitness trainers do not have to be certified, it helps establish your credentials and validates your knowledge of the business.

There is little overhead involved in becoming a personal trainer. Aside from business cards, education expenses, and certification fees, much of your hourly fee is profit. Some personal trainers further supplement their incomes by providing space planning consultation for in-home gyms.

On a less complicated level, it is possible to advertise yourself as a "workout partner" instead of a personal trainer. As a workout partner you are merely there to exercise alongside your customer and inspire them to keep going. Fees for workout partners would be far lower ($6 to $10 an hour), but you would only be selling your enthusiasm and inspiration, not your knowledge and skill in designing a training program.

Special Occasion Sign Rentals

Birthdays, anniversaries, weddings, job promotions, births, and all manner of noteworthy occasions can be celebrated in high style with a "special occasion sign" planted on the recipient's front lawn. Part-time entrepreneur Dean Handy rents his Yard Cards to folks who want a high-profile celebration. "With the birth announcements, it is usually the dad who orders the sign. Fortieth birthdays and the like, it is bound to be either the wife or a couple of his friends playing a trick." Dean has an inventory of 30 signs for various occasions, and each one of the signs rents for $25 a day, $35 for three days, or $50 for the whole week. The cost includes delivery, installation, and pick-up, as well as a personalized message painted on the sign. The big wooden signs are all handmade by Dean, based on drawings that an artist does for him. He blows the design up and traces it onto the wood and then paints in the design himself. Big bunny rabbits for birthdays and birth announcements, a large Grim Reaper popular for 30th and 40th birthdays, teddy bears, giraffes, and a carousel horse are among the signs that Dean rents out. Although Dean is an independent operator who created his business from scratch, there is a nationwide sign-rental franchise company that specializes in large storks for birth announcements, so he stays away from storks.

The special occasion sign business is well-suited for weekend entrepreneurs. "Most rentals do take place on the weekends," Dean told me. "People like to have the signs out front during birthday parties and that is generally when they are held."

When starting out, Dean was able to generate business right away because he worked on his signs on his own front lawn and attracted a lot of attention from passersby. He also plants the signs in his own front yard on occasion, but recommends against overdoing it to avoid annoying your neighbors. He has tried several different methods of advertising and marketing—advertising, flyers in card stores, and even displays at bridal fairs. Business has its ups and downs, but he averages about 20 sign rentals a month.

Dean has some good advice for weekend entrepreneurs who think that their area could support this type of business—plan carefully! "Draw up a business plan that takes all aspects of the business into consideration, everything from financing to marketing. Once you draw up your plan, stick with it! If you don't have a business plan or outline you will stray from your original intentions very quickly. Even though this is a part-time business, take it seriously and make sure that you allot enough of your time and energy to it."

Teaching Special Classes

Do you have a skill, hobby, or talent that others would really like to learn? A great way to make weekend money is to teach private classes to small groups of people. Successful small classes can be held on a variety of topics—creative writing, foreign languages, literary and historical topics, cooking, wood-working, crafts, even etiquette! Many years ago I taught a class on self-publishing to a group of ten people who had each paid $45 for an afternoon. I rented a room in a community center for $30 an afternoon and the remaining $420 was profit! The only reason that I have not continued to teach is that I do not enjoy standing in front of a room full of strangers. If you are shy, this is not a SAM for you. But for those who are bold enough, teaching can be a very rewarding experience, both emotionally and financially. "Our society is going through an exciting explosion in lifelong learning. More people than ever are becoming involved in classes and educational events, for personal reasons and for professional reasons," says William Draves, founder and Director of the Learning Resources Network.

Novelist and screenwriter (*Inside Moves*) Todd Walton teaches a six-week course in creative writing to groups of eight for the modest sum of $122. Classes are held in his living room every Wednesday night. He provides soft pillows and all the Chinese tea you can drink; students bring their own paper and pens. His classes are so popular that he no longer has to advertise, the word of mouth is so tremendous that a long waiting list exists for months in advance.

Bart Brodsky, founder of Open Exchange in Berkeley, California, says that the opportunities for teachers and topics are endless. "The YMCAs, exercise salons, dance studios, New Age meditation retreats, and special interest clubs are all vying for a piece of the educational pie. The range and the functions of the activities—intellectual, social, ethical, and spiritual, are beyond the scope of any one, 1,000, or 10,000 providers to handle." So find your teaching niche and get going!

Few things could be as simple as teaching a class. Once you have determined that you have knowledge that other folks would pay to learn (or you go out and learn something specifically so that you can make extra money teaching it to others) follow a few short simple steps:

1. Find a location in which to hold the class. Your own home would be the least expensive, of course, but it might not be the most desir-

able. Take a good, hard look at your surroundings and try to see them from the standpoint of a complete stranger who has arrived to take a class. Would you be delighted at the location, or dismayed? If you do not honestly think that strangers would be delighted to spend several hours in your living room, then you must rent a location. Churches and schools are good places to look; they often have community rooms which can be rented for a short period of time for a modest sum. Make sure that the price of the room includes use of the chairs! A blackboard on the wall or an overhead projector might also be needed, depending on your teaching methods.

2. Advertise for students. Small community newspapers are ideal, as are free bulletin boards in bookstores, community centers, or wherever else your potential students might go. Many communities have organized learning programs like The Learning Annex in New York and San Francisco, and Open Exchange in Berkeley. These programs are always on the lookout for new and interesting courses to offer and are always open to hearing new ideas. They will take a large percentage of your class fee, but it is a great way to get started.

3. Plan your curriculum. Make sure that you have enough to talk about for the entire class. It takes an awful lot of talking to fill up two or three hours. Plan your class in such a way that there are many points at which you can stop and open it up for students' questions. Students expect learning in this type of a class to be quick, informative, and fun. Prepare handouts and other materials that your students can examine during class and take home afterwards. Prepare exercises that the whole class can do. Todd Walton's creative writing class consists primarily of short exercises that he has developed to spur creativity in his own work. The students do the exercises in the quiet of his living room, take a break, then read their work aloud.

4. Try to anticipate what problems might occur and be prepared to deal with them. Make sure you have a back-up plan in case something goes wrong with your scheduled location, or for some reason you need to reschedule the date and time of your class.

5. Teach! With each class you teach you will learn something new, enabling you to refine and improve your class continuously. You may soon find that you can teach a more advanced level of the same class, which will give you an opportunity to work with the same students all over again. If you did a good job with the beginner-level class they will be happy to learn from you once more. It is useful to hand out an

anonymous evaluation form at the end of your class so that you will instantly have feedback from your students, good or bad. This will help you spot problems and take steps to improve for the next group.

Prices for classes vary widely. To decide your price, consider the following: How well do I know my subject? How professional are my teaching skills? How difficult is it to obtain this knowledge? Always start with a modest price for your first few classes; $25 for an afternoon class would be acceptable. Another way to get started is to offer a "free introductory class" as a way to get potential students interested. If you start modestly, once you become comfortable with your topic and start to see positive feedback from your students, you may be justified in raising your price. Before you commit to a particular price, check the competition to see if similar classes are being offered and at what rate. Take your expenses and costs into consideration as well.

A good basic book on this subject is:

> *The Teaching Marketplace: Make Money with Freelance*
> *Teaching, Corporate Trainings, and On the Lecture Circuit*
> Bart Brodsky and Janet Geis
> Community Resource Institute Press
> (510) 525-9663
> $14.95

Freelance Publicity for Small Businesses

You might have noticed that I talk a lot about the need for weekend businesses to draw attention to themselves through free publicity. Publicity, as opposed to paid advertising, is the single most effective way for just about any business, large or small, to draw new clients and customers. A five-minute spot on the television news that highlights a newly introduced product, a funny description of your business by a disc jockey during the morning drive—this kind of exposure adds up to real money. Where do small businesspeople turn if they don't know how to generate this kind of free publicity on their own? Why, to a freelance publicist, of course.

Most freelance publicists got their training one of four ways:

1. They once held a job doing publicity for a large company or small business;
2. They were involved with a volunteer organization that needed help with publicity and no one else was willing to give it a try;
3. Former business owners themselves, they learned the hard way how to get publicity;
4. Interested in the idea, they went out and bought a book on publicity to learn how it works.

Most of you will fall into the last category. There are many books available that can help you learn the basics of publicity, from writing an effective press release to all of the etiquette involved in pitching an idea for a story. These books will tell you how to find the information that is critical to a publicist—the names, addresses, and phone numbers of newspaper editors, magazine editors, radio and television producers. Some day you might have occasion to pitch your client to the Oprah Winfrey Show (although they receive hundreds of such pitches each week)!

Laura Lewis worked for many years as publicity manager for a book publishing company before deciding to stay home full-time with her children. Once the children started preschool, however, she found she had enough extra time to start up a small business doing freelance publicity. "My skills were a bit rusty at that point," she told me, "so I did go out and buy the most recent books on the topic to see if anything had changed." Once she refreshed her knowledge she signed up her first client—a local charity. Laura charges $30 an hour for the time she spends writing press releases, sending them to local newspapers, magazines, and television stations, and making follow-up calls to editors and producers to ask if they would like to speak to her client. "What kind of skill or talent does it take to be a publicist? You have to be a bit pushy, able to call a complete stranger and not be intimidated by the fact that they work for a TV station or a newspaper. Don't be obnoxious, of course, but you do have to be quietly persistent in your efforts. And if a good story comes out of the press release you sent them, they will be happy to hear from you again. Always keep in mind that these folks are actively looking for story ideas, and try to develop the best angle you can."

Who needs publicity? Just about any business or organization is a potential client. Once you are able to get some media coverage for your first client you can do a bit of bragging and use that to interest new clients!

Here is a quick description of how a freelance publicist helped a small business get great publicity in the newspaper.

David Brown, a professional photographer in Cincinnati, took a beautiful photo for a poster that the post office wanted to use to encourage letter writing. The photo was a soft-focus photo of his wife's hands. She was holding a fancy writing pen, and resting her hand on a stack of letters that had yellowed with age. Gin Sander, a friend of David's with a background in publicity, listened to his description of how he set the shot up using the love letters that his own parents had exchanged during World War II and seized upon that as an angle for a possible newspaper story. She wrote up a short press release describing the touching circumstances behind the photo and sent it off to the major newspapers. Within two weeks there was a large reproduction of David's photo in the newspaper along with a short story. Both David and his client, the U.S. Post Office, were pleased with the publicity.

Here is a selection of books that will help you understand how to do publicity for small businesses:

Getting Publicity: The Very Best Book for Your
Small Business
Tana Fletcher and Julia Rockler
Self Counsel Press
$14.95

Publicity Kit: A Complete Guide for Entrepreneurs, Small
Businesses, and Nonprofit Organizations
Jeanette Smith
John Wiley and Sons
$17.95

Home Tutoring

Not every parent has strong skills in math, English, or science. If those were your best topics in school you might be able to start up a profitable home-tutoring business. How exactly do you tutor? Sit down right next to the child and help them puzzle out their homework assignments. Tutoring can be done in the child's home or in your home, depending on the parent's preference.

Tutors find their clients many ways, including running small ads in parenting newspapers and newsletters, connecting with schools and teachers, and talking their services up to local parents. Tutors are paid an hourly rate, which varies from community to community. The average is $10 an hour.

With the rise in home-schooling there might be a corresponding need for tutors in topics that home-schoolers don't feel comfortable teaching to their children. Keep your eyes open for ways to connect with the home-schoolers in your neighborhood.

Feng Shui Consultant

Starr Hughes is a high school teacher who felt the need to do something different in her life. "I just felt a big hole, a big need that wasn't being met." She began to read books on different types of religions and beliefs, and when she first read about feng shui it all seemed to fall into place.

Feng shui literally means "wind and water" and is an ancient Chinese belief that there is a proper way to place things in your house to attract luck, prosperity, and wealth. A belief in feng shui has begun to grow dramatically in the past years, and even large corporations are starting to call on feng shui consultants to examine their interior layout and make suggestions on placement of furniture, mirrors, and plants to encourage prosperity.

How do you become a feng shui consultant? Starr read every book on the topic that she could find and began to attend lectures in her area. Once she felt that she had sufficient understanding of the topic, she felt comfortable advising others. "I charge $150 for a complete consultation. I go to the client's home and examine the entire house and property and make suggestions about how things could be rearranged in order to attract better luck."

Two good books to help you get started with feng shui are:

Feng Shui Made Easy
William Spear
Harper Collins
$16

Feng Shui Handbook
Master Lam Kam Chuen
Henry Holt
$16.95

Family History Videos and Scrapbooks

Interest in family histories is sweeping the nation, with an increase in everything from organized family reunions to scrapbooks, computer-generated genealogies, and elaborately filmed oral histories from the older members of the family. There are two ways to generate an extra income from this trend. The first is to become affiliated with one of the national companies that sell archival scrapbook supplies, like Creative Memories. Creative Memories will help you create your own home-based business, offering the classes and materials necessary for putting together archival-quality photo albums certain to last for many future generations.

After making her own photo albums for the last four years, Mimi Trousil of Lafayette, Colorado, became a consultant with Creative Memories and now teaches classes and sells the album materials. "It doesn't cost too much to get started, $300 in inventory is the minimum. But if you are really going to work this as a business you would need to buy more like $1,000 in inventory to get started. I try to have one class a week, so I really move product quickly." Unlike cosmetics companies or kitchenware companies that sell through consultants, Creative Memories calls their evening get-togethers "classes" instead of "parties." "The difference," Mimi says, "is that you can come to a Creative Memories class and learn a great deal about proper photo mounting and storage, journaling, layout, and other archival skills. You don't have to buy anything if you don't want to. It will still have been time well spent learning about how to put good photo albums together." To learn more about Creative Memories, call (800) 468-9335 and they will gladly mail information.

Rhoda Lewis and Phyllis Massing are interested in helping folks preserve family memories through a different medium. They use videotape. Their company, Life Stories, in Encino, California, charges customers up to $2,500 for a professional video biography that incorporates music and still photos along with a taped interview. They urge their customers to be fully prepared for the interview, to go back and look at high school yearbooks, favorite keepsakes, military records, and anything else that will help sharpen the memories and make for a compelling video interview. After starting out doing their own camera work, they realized that achieving professional-quality sound was tricky and they now hire professional videographers to accompany them to the interviews. They have written a book that will tell you how to conduct an interview and produce a family video:

From Generation to Generation
Rhoda Lewis and Phyllis Massing

To order a copy, send $25 (includes shipping and handling) to:

Life Stories
16161 Ventura Blvd., Suite 634
Encino, CA 91436

Sports Videographer

Here is a camcorder-related business idea. I learned about this type of business while drinking coffee in a cafe in Newport Beach, California. Always on the lookout for new ideas, I make it a habit to read the local bulletin boards to see if anyone is advertising anything unusual and, yes, that day I found someone! A small, carefully printed 3×5 card advertised the availability of a local woman who would, for a fee, come out to the beach with local surfers and videotape them surfing. Hey, what a great way to spend a morning! Surfers, skiers, snowboarders, skateboarders—who wouldn't want a tape of themselves performing their favorite pastime? Serious athletes will want the tapes to critique their technique; others just want a good-looking record of themselves to capture the moment.

Start by videotaping your kids or friends playing sports and get the hang of how to go about this. Zoom techniques are critical, and you want to be able to deliver a product with a well-crafted, professional look by varying shots between long distance and close up. Books on home video techniques will give you ideas on how to add music and voice-over commentary to the tape. Surfers and skateboarders might request their favorite song be dubbed onto the tape for added effect.

After you have developed your technique to the point that you feel comfortable selling the finished product, find your potential customers. Identify the local hangouts for surfers, skateboarders, skiers, and other extreme sports enthusiasts. Just as I stumbled across a small card posted at a cafe, this is the way that you might start getting your message out. Make up a small flyer, business card, or printed notice that explains what you do and how much it costs. Posting this notice should get you the first few clients, and if they are pleased with your product, they will spread the word to friends.

A professional, finished, 15-minute sports video should cost in the $75 range, not including the cost of videotape.

Expert Toy Assembly

Are you the one your friends always call for help with a complicated toy assembly? Does your phone ring late at night on Christmas Eve with frustrated questions as parents all across town struggle to put together gifts at the last minute? Two California men, Dick Bleu and Dan Mateer, started a part-time specialty business called Some Assembly Required to help parents who don't know which way to turn a screwdriver. A toy assembly business works best on a seasonal basis, with Christmas being the main season.

How will you let parents know about your availability as a toy assembler for hire? The best way would be an article in the local newspaper, or perhaps the local free parenting newspaper. A business like this, particularly one run by a woman, would make a great article. Radio stations and television stations would consider this as topic for a story, so go after free publicity right after Thanksgiving signals the start of the shopping/toy assembly season. Another way to let parents know about your services is to print up flyers with information about your business and leaflet the cars parked at large toy stores.

Charge a minimum of $20 for simple assembly, and a higher fee for more complex jobs. Keep in mind that your price should not be too outrageous. Parents who have just paid a healthy sum for a toy or bicycle will have second thoughts and quickly consider returning the merchandise if it costs them too much to have someone else assemble it for them!

Thinking It Through

For most of the business ideas detailed here you must possess one important element—creativity. There are no books, no business plans that you can read to figure out how to make them succeed. Large doses of passion, creativity, and imagination will come in handy. If you do not think you could succeed in a business that you will to a great extent be creating on your own, these are not the ideas for you. Better to stick to staid, tried-and-true businesses such as those found in "Back to Basics" or "Old-Fashioned Money."

Publicity is a key element in the success of these businesses, and you must ask yourself if you want publicity. Not everyone feels comfortable talking to the press, giving radio interviews, or standing in front of a television camera. The press would love to write a story about someone with a holistic housecleaning business, or someone who gives tours of the local graveyard, and if you thrive on attention maybe you have what it takes. If you are not comfortable in the spotlight, one possibility is to take on a partner; perhaps your spouse or one of your children would enjoy handling the publicity and meet-the-press side of things.

To learn more about how to get free publicity for yourself or your business, you might take a look at:

> *Publicity Kit: A Complete Guide for Entrepreneurs, Small*
> *Businesses, and Nonprofit Organizations*
> Jeanette Smith
> John Wiley and Sons
> $17.95

Take a chance on some of these oddball ideas. Some of the most successful people in the world are businesspeople who managed to make a quirky business idea work in a big way. And remember one of life's old rules: The biggest rewards lie at the end of the biggest risks!

Chapter Six

Available Talent— Opportunities for Artists, Musicians, and Writers

For those lucky enough to be gifted with artistic or musical talent, there are many creative ways to earn an extra income. Why not work all week long in a straight-laced business environment, decked out in business suit and pumps, then break loose on weekends and indulge your creative pursuits for extra cash! What a terrific way to balance all of your needs and talents.

Art Parties/One-Night-Only Galleries

Over the summer I received a beautiful invitation to a garden party. Knowing what a lovely home and backyard my friend had, I eagerly made plans to attend. Once I walked into the garden on the afternoon of the party, however, I began to notice something unusual—scattered around the gravel walkway were small tables filled with interesting pieces of art for sale. My friend Julia was throwing an art party!

"I was having coffee with several of my friends from the art college," she told me later, "and we were bemoaning the fact that it is so hard to make any money as an artist. It is hard to get a gallery to represent you, and even if you are represented you will probably only get to have a showing of your art every other year or so. The rest of the time your work just gathers dust in the back room of the gallery. So we had a group brainstorm. Why not have our own Saturday afternoon show and sale combined with a summer garden party? Each of us would have a section of the garden in which we could build our own display area. We would all pitch in together to combine names for the mailing list. We also shared expenses for the food, drinks, and invitation printing and mailing."

It was a magical setting. Off among the daisy beds was a display of African sculpture; large oil paintings were hung against the white-washed fence. Inside the house Julia displayed her ceramic sculptures of shoes and purses, each piece artfully nestled in draped cloth. Very quickly I spent $60 on one of Julia's sculptures, and $20 on a set of ceramic mugs made by another local artist. I noticed that I was by no means the only one buying art; many of the guests wandered the paths with their arms clutching new purchases. In addition to buying some wonderful art, it was a fine afternoon party with lots of music, tasty food, and interesting guests. "It was simple to plan, enjoyable to attend, and we all ended up selling a great deal of art. We think it will be an annual event," Julia told me afterwards. I think I will be there for the next one, too!

Another version of the art party is a "one-night-only" gallery. Where an art party is a casual outdoors affair, a one-night-only gallery has more of an "event" feel and is a larger undertaking. To stage one, you must first find a suitable empty gallery space. A successful Sacramento art promoter borrows friend's large apartments for his one-night events. Large rooms with plain white walls work best; it is also important to remove previous art and push excess furniture into a spare room to create a suitable gallery feel and have room for guests. A terrific time to approach people about using their house or apartment is just before they move out because the furniture will be gone and the owner will not be inconvenienced.

Postcards are a good and inexpensive way to alert art lovers about your event. Mail them to your friends and supporters, and also to potential collectors and art lovers. Members of the local museum? Patrons of other galleries?

Send press releases about your one-night-only gallery to local newspapers and ask them to list it on the events page. This is a free service in most newspapers and if they are intrigued by your event, they might just send a reporter to cover it!

Calligraphy

Calligraphy is the art of beautiful handwriting, something that few of us possess. Over the centuries a highly stylized version of calligraphy has developed and those who have mastered it or can develop the talent will find that they have a highly marketable skill.

The biggest demand for custom calligraphers is handaddressing wedding invitations or other event announcements. Calligraphers can alert local invitation printers that their services are for hire to attract business; friendly printers may even let you leave a brochure or flyer about your services on their counter. Hand-addressing wedding invitations is very timeconsuming. Once you determine how many envelopes you can address in an hour you should set your rates so that you make at least $30 an hour. For instance, if you discover that you can address 50 cards an hour, then charge $60 to address 100 wedding invitations. Not too shabby for two hours' work! You must be very careful when addressing wedding invitations though. Since most people only print close to the number they plan to send out, you have a very small margin of error.

Besides addressing invitations, another need for beautifully hand-lettered work can be found in awards, proclamations, and special recognitions. Many corporations and community organizations hand out special awards to employees and members who deserve special recognition. The awards are that much more meaningful when the recipient's name and achievement is recorded in graceful calligraphy. You should have a simple fee structure for these assignments: $25 per award would be reasonable. One good way to get the word of your skills out to businesses and organizations is to send beautifully lettered notes to public affairs and public relations offices of large companies.

Clowns, Puppet Shows, and Magicians

Are you always the center of attention at family gatherings? Famous for your silly act at office parties? Maybe you should take up clowning as a part-time profession! Pansy Potts did, in a career move that she calls "serendipity." Clowns are in great demand on weekends at children's parties, Christmas shows, and company picnics. Everybody loves a clown, and if you really love children (no one should try this if they don't) you will also love the $80 an hour that clowns command for performances!

Pansy worked at many things before becoming a weekend clown, but nothing was as satisfying. She encourages women in particular to take up clowning. "Clowns can be kind of scary to young children and women clowns are smaller and not so intimidating." In addition to her clown act, she tells stories, makes balloon animals, and stages a puppet show. And where did she learn to do all of this? Clown college! For the serious student of clowning, La Crosse University in La Crosse, Wisconsin, offers clown classes in the summer. Their teachers are the very same clowning instructors who teach at Ringling Brothers Clown College in Florida. Once you learn the basics, you can stay ahead of the competition and keep your skills sharp by joining Clowns International to continue training and learning.

Becoming a "community clown" (instead of a circus clown) can be financially and emotionally rewarding, but Pansy warns that start-up costs can be high. Investing in an outfit and professional makeup is expensive, as is advertising for clients. "It doesn't happen all at once," Pansy says. "It might take six months before you actually start to see some money. Polish your skills in the meantime by performing for free at local convalescent homes and hospitals."

To learn more about becoming a clown and the opportunities available for weekend clowning, you might subscribe to:

Clowns of America
Calliope
P.O. Box 570
Lake Jackson, TX 77566-0570

Wavy Gravy, a long-time '60s proponent of clowning around, teaches special one-week sessions for adults who want to learn the fine art of clowning. For information, contact him at:

Camp Winnarainbow
Circus and Performing Arts Camp
1301 Henry St.
Berkeley, CA 94709
(510) 525-4304

Puppets

"Puppetry is an art form," Mary Charles told me, "and if properly learned it can also become a very lucrative one." Mary's part-time puppet company, Puppets Unlimited, ran a thriving birthday party business in Hawaii. In addition to birthday parties, she suggests incorporating educational materials like local legends and myths into your puppet shows as a way to enter into the school visit market. At an average of $100 for an afternoon show, puppet shows can provide a tidy source of extra money.

To learn puppetry, Mary suggests that you attend as many shows as you can to get a sense of what other local puppeteers are doing. There are national puppetry conventions held annually that include workshops and seminars on making puppets, writing scripts, and performance techniques. Contact the Puppeteers of America for more information. The Puppeteers of America also publish the *Puppetry Journal,* to help keep you informed of goings-on in the puppetry community.

Magician

"I first learned magic when I was a kid. I was on crutches for several years, and so instead of playing sports I taught myself to perform magic tricks," Bill Devon told me. A full-time parking enforcement officer, Bill gets a lot of kicks and a steady source of extra income by working as a magician. "Most private birthday parties I charge $75 a show, but for a larger business or organization my rate is more like $150. On average I do about four shows a month." In addition to birthday parties, he does shows at fairs, on cruises, reunions, or community events. Having been in the magic business for many years, referrals bring many of the jobs his way, and he also runs small ads in community papers.

How do you become a paid magician? Bill learned from books and by exchanging ideas with other magicians. "Other magicians will help you out. It is a friendly fraternity of sorts," he says. To find other magicians in your area, check out your local magic store. They should be able to put you in contact with the local chapter of the IBM—the International Brotherhood of Magicians. Pull out that old pack of playing cards and start practicing!

Children's Party Specialist

Not ready to entertain the world as a magician, puppeteer, or clown, but still like to attend children's high-energy birthday parties? Why not be the person in charge of arranging them! "ATTENTION BUSY PARENTS," read an ad I saw in a parenting newspaper. The ad went on to describe this enterprising woman's availability as a birthday party organizer—everything from booking entertainment to ordering the cake to organizing and running the children's games, and even the clean-up afterwards! Such a deal.

Finding clients and spreading the word about your services as a party organizer should be simple. Not only can you connect and pass the word to other parents in your neighborhood, church, or place of work, but this is an ideal angle for a story in your local newspaper.

Another way to earn extra money from children's birthday parties is by putting together "party boxes" for theme parties. The boxes contain everything from the plates, napkins, and glasses down to the plastic beads you would need for, say, a pirate theme party. The service you are performing is to save a busy parent the job of having to drive around town picking up every little thing for Junior's party. Take a look around your area to see if anyone else is performing these kinds of services, and if not, go for it!

Custom Murals and Children's Furniture

"I majored in art in college," Sandy Hoover told me, "but I never really did anything with it. I went to work as a landscaper and did that for several years. Then my sister asked me to paint a mural on the wall in her new baby's room, and I enjoyed it so much that I decided to get back into art." Sandy's business, Wall Antics, specializes in small or large custom murals for children's rooms. She paints one or two murals a month, charging anywhere from $500 to $1,500, depending on the size and the complexity of the design.

Many of her jobs have come from word-of-mouth, but she also tries to work with local interior decorators for referrals, and has on occasion advertised in newsletters catering to parents of small children. Each mural takes several weeks to complete, working primarily on weekends when the homeowner is around. "I am bonded with personal liability," Sandy says, "in case I spill paint all over their carpet or something. I really recommend covering yourself that way! Don't take chances."

Connecticut-based artist Elizabeth Katz also advertises her mural painting company, adrawables, in small parenting magazines. A full-time mother, she sets aside two days a week to market her murals to schools, showcase homes, and hospitals. "I let schools know that I am available to paint murals in the library, gym, cafeteria, or wherever else the walls need to be livened up!" Elizabeth majored in art history in college and spent several years working in publishing before the birth of her son, Ben. She hasn't yet painted a mural in his room, but has given him another of her products—a custom-painted bureau. "I do more furniture than murals right now," she explained. "Rocking chairs, toy chests, stools, and small table and chair sets. No one has asked to have a bed painted, though. Most parents want the furniture painted to match the wallpaper or the curtains."

Painted children's furniture and custom room murals are growing in popularity as Baby Boomers become parents themselves. Creating a weekend pursuit that caters to this ever-growing trend will assure extra income for years to come. Elizabeth recommends placing samples of your painted furniture in children's clothing stores to interest potential customers.

Faux Finishing

You've seen it in countless lifestyle magazines: walls that look like marble when in fact they are not. "Faux" is French for "fake," but it does sound so much nicer in French, doesn't it? Learning how to apply your artistic talents to painting faux finishes can add very real money to your bank account. From marbling techniques to mottled and sponged surfaces, these skills are in great demand by home remodelers, interior designers, and house painters.

If you already possess the basic skills of painting, it will not be hard for you to master these techniques. Jocasta Innes, the queen of decorating with paint, has written a number of books that will help you learn. There are kits you can purchase in art supply stores, but if you plan to ply this skill professionally you need to know how to do it without using expensive products from a kit. Check to see if your local art store teaches classes in faux painting techniques.

This is a highly paid skill, and you should first check to see if anyone else in your community is offering these services. If so, price your services accordingly, a little bit lower than the competition. Once you gain skill and word spreads among decorators (your best advertisement) you should be able to raise your prices. Make sure that you are getting at least $20 an hour for your time, and that customers understand that they buy the paint. You will have to use your own special small brushes.

The New Decorator's Handbook: Decorative Paint
Techniques for Every Room
Jocasta Innes
HarperCollins
$23

Face Painting

Cheeks painted with rainbows, clouds, and stars were standard fare at '60s love-ins and Grateful Dead concerts and fell from popularity for a few decades. But like platform shoes and bell-bottom jeans, they're back. Take a look at the faces of small children at any large public event like a county fair or an amusement park and you will see tiny Barneys and Batmen, happy faces (they're back too!), and rainbows painted on almost everyone. An artist with painting skills can easily find weekend work as a freelance face painter to meet the demands of these young art patrons.

"I make $100 an afternoon," says Cathleen Swanson, "depending on what kind of event it is. If it is a charity event I might charge less, but if it is a big craft fair or other for-profit event then I do ask $100." Event organizers pay for the face painter's services and children line up and have their faces decorated for free. "Parents love it, and it makes the children feel very special," Cathleen says. A substitute teacher during the week, Cathleen only works one or two days a month as a face painter. Summer months are the most active as there are more events held then. In addition to outdoor events like fairs and concerts, face painters also work at events sponsored by city parks and recreation departments. Birthday parties and company picnics like to have face painters around for the kids. Cathleen finds work by contacting the public relations departments at hospitals to let them know she is available on Saturdays and Sundays to paint faces at parties and community "wellness" fairs, and also pays close attention to advertisements about big events. She makes it a point to call the organizers of the event to inquire about hiring. "Radio stations are also a prime source for work," she says. "They run many outdoor promotions and events that use face painters as part of the entertainment."

Supplies are few, just several brushes and a good selection of colors. Cathleen uses a brand of water-based theatrical paint from Germany called Kryolon, available at costume and theatrical stores, and sometimes found in art supply or hobby stores as well. "Most kids ask for whatever cartoon character happens to be popular, Disney or movie characters like Batman. I encourage them to want things from nature like fish, insects, or flowers. A very popular trick is to paint their entire face to look like a lion or a cat. They love it."

Face painting seems most popular among small children, but a trend is catching on with adults that a talented face painter could latch onto—temporary tattoos. More detailed and time-consuming work, but a great way to make money! Using the same water-based theatrical paint but with smaller, finer brushes, a talented painter could charge up to $25 per tattoo. Not a bad way to make extra money on a sunny afternoon.

Singing Christmas Carols

Organizing a professional caroling group is a great seasonal business for singers. A recent *Money* magazine article on home-based businesses profiled one couple who make an extra $30,000 a year with their business, the Living Christmas Card. Caroling groups can charge several hundred dollars an hour for their custom holiday performances and are busy throughout the Christmas season at Rotary luncheons, retail stores, and malls.

Organizing a professional-quality vocal group is the first hurdle, but once you find your fellow singers and begin a strict regime of practice sessions to get lungs and lyrics in shape for the holiday season you will have to turn your attention to marketing. Sheri Marshall, who owns Living Christmas Card with her husband Craig, devotes two days a week to marketing their group to booking agents. Contact community groups, rental halls, retail stores, and large malls to alert them that your group is available. Your group will stand out all the more if you develop a unique sound, perhaps a "doo wop" approach to traditional Christmas tunes or a strictly Medieval sound, anything to set you apart from other singing groups in your area.

House Portraits and Custom Stationery

I grew up on a street lined with old family homes on one side and a vast green park on the other. It was a terrific place for a kid to roam, and it was also fertile ground for enterprising artists with architectural rendering skills. Once every two or three years the doorbell would ring and a smiling artist would suggest that my folks engage their services to sketch, paint, or photograph our house. The prices ranged from $150 for a photograph (my parents declined) to $85 for a pen-and-ink sketch (my parents agreed). The woman who successfully sold her artistic talent came prepared with a sample book of portraits that she had done in other towns and neighborhoods. After shaking hands on the deal, she agreed to return the following day to render the portrait.

For several hours she sat perched on a stool at the side of the driveway as she carefully studied each element of the house and translated it as simply and elegantly as she could onto her sketch pad. At the end of the afternoon she rang the doorbell again and proudly presented my parents with her work, an 8-by-10-inch pen-and-ink drawing of their house—trees and all. Accepting the check for her efforts, she suggested that in addition to framing the drawing and displaying it on a wall, they might want to take it to a printer and have custom stationery made. An excellent idea, they agreed, and for the last few years whenever I am in trouble I have been receiving terse notes from my mother on custom folded note cards imprinted on the front with the portrait of their house. It tends to soften the blow . . . .

Wealthy neighborhoods are prime areas in which to sell house portraits, but more modest areas might also be good scouting ground. To get started, first do several portraits of a friend's home, or the homes of strangers (who knows, perhaps you can sell it to them once you get established!). Try several different architectural styles to display your range. Assemble samples of your work in a handsome and expensive-looking photo album, print up some business cards, decide on your price, put on professional clothes for your initial contacts, and start pounding the pavement. Make certain that your price is within reason: Don't price yourself too high or you will never get this business off the ground.

Instead of painting or drawing a straight portrait, you might also suggest that you could produce a snowy winter setting for the portrait to use for custom Christmas cards. This is certain to appeal to well-heeled homeowners hoping to impress their friends at the holidays! Charge a bit more to "winterize" the scene.

Custom house portraits are also of interest to real estate agents looking for an inexpensive way to spruce up a marketing brochure for a particular property. Including a small drawing or sketch of the house for sale is a classy touch, and less expensive to print than a photo. Once you become an experienced house portrait artist consider making your own flyer or brochure and dropping it off at realty offices to attract more work. What better way to spend a weekend than selling a portrait or two?

Printmakers and silk-screen artists can also sell custom stationery based on houses. The project would take more time than a three-hour sketch, but would be just as appealing. With this type of product you would be agreeing to deliver designed and printed cards or stationery instead of just a simple portrait. Consider your prices carefully. You must find a price for 200 or more custom-designed and printed cards that will be both affordable for a customer and profitable for you. I spoke to an enterprising art student who warned that this is "labor intensive," but ultimately worth the effort.

If your artistic talent does not lend itself to house portraits, consider animal portraits. Many pet owners are devoted to their animals, in life and in death, and are willing to pay large sums of money to have their beloved pet rendered on canvas. This work is best done from a photograph, as animals are seldom cooperative about sitting still.

Mobile Art Gallery

Artist Kathy Lee had an idea—why not bring her artwork right to people's homes and offices so that they could make their selections knowing what looked good hanging on the walls? And why not take the work of other artists along with her while she made her rounds? With that idea a new part-time business was born, a mobile art gallery.

"I'm a potter, but other than my stuff I was only willing to sell works-on-paper. Paintings and prints are relatively easy to transport, pottery and sculpture are not! I wanted to design the whole business to fit in the back seat of my car, and so that was what I focused on. Besides my own art, I represented the work of twenty other artists." Rather than take 50 percent or more of the selling price like a standard gallery, Kathy kept 40 percent of the proceeds from the other artists' work. The artists were pleased to get a greater percentage, and also pleased at Kathy's gung-ho attitude toward finding new clients for their art.

Her first step was to join the local Chamber of Commerce to be able to attend the "business mixer" functions offered to members. "I met a lot of clients that way. I would put on my most businesslike outfit and chat up the executives. Eventually the conversation would get around to what I did, and in many cases I walked away with an appointment to come to their office or home and show the art. Art in an office projects an air of sophistication, but to tell you the truth most of the businesspeople that I talked to were pretty intimidated by the thought of going into a gallery to make a purchase. It can be kind of scary. Once they realized that I would bring the art to them, they were really relieved." In addition to her activities with the Chamber of Commerce, Kathy advertised in local business newspapers and publications, and received many referrals from satisfied clients.

Most of the art that Kathy had for sale was priced in the $200 to $400 range, but she also handled more expensive pieces. Offering layaway terms to her clients was another bonus, although she did not deliver the piece until the account was fully settled. "It is easy for people to make up their minds right away if you are standing right in their living room or office with the piece hanging on the wall. It looks good, they can afford it, so why not buy?"

A mobile art gallery is a perfect SAM for a working artist. You determine your own selling hours, and are completely free to work on your own art whenever you want. Most of your clients will want you to come in the evening or late in the afternoon for office appointments. (Make sure that you find out in advance how many decision-makers there are in the home or office, and that all will be available!) Once you begin to set original prints and paintings out that catch their eye, you are on your way to a sale!

Start-up costs are low for a business like this. In addition to joining the chamber, Kathy had business cards made. "The chamber membership was expensive," she warns, "but it really did pay off." Another advantage to a mobile art gallery is the fact that there really is no overhead. You are not paying rent on a fancy retail space hoping that art-buying customers will wander in by chance; you can store the arts and crafts in an extra bedroom or closet until it is time for the next appointment. You are also providing a real service for your fellow artists—most artists are more creative than organized, and so a talented person with the organizational skills to pull this off is a real treasure and will find it easy to interest artists in representation. "I recommend it," says Kathy Lee. "It works for me."

Children's Pen Pal

A tiny ad in the *New Yorker* magazine tipped me off to a wonderful business idea for writers—letter writing to children! Who doesn't remember the thrill of receiving a letter (addressed to ME!) as a young child. Didn't that make you feel important and grown-up? So little letter writing goes on nowadays, and most of what we receive in the mail is not personal correspondence, but junk mail. Unless children are lucky enough to have grandparents who cling to the ways of paper and pen in our e-mail times, chances are that many children will never receive a letter at all.

Advertise your availability as a paid pen pal correspondent for children! The ad in the magazine might read: "Children's writer and illustrator seeks correspondents aged 6 to 12. One year of interactive, illustrated letters plus exquisite writing supplies. $36.95 & $3.50 s/h." What a treat it would be for a child to receive a beautiful letter! Concentrate on presentation as well as content so that each letter is itself a work of art.

Thinking It Through

Before you turn your talents into a business, you must first ask yourself the same sorts of questions that I recommended for crafters—can you handle rejection? Not everyone will wholeheartedly embrace your artistic or musical style; taste is not universal. How will you feel if a potential customer takes one look at the samples of custom house portraits that you have put together so carefully and says, "Gee, you want me to pay money for that? Get real!" You must learn not to take these rejections personally. It is all in a day's work and many an acclaimed artist has had his or her work ridiculed.

Your artwork might also be a private pleasure that you won't enjoy selling. Some artists truly feel that they are "prostituting" their talent by trying to pander to a broad audience. Decide if you will feel comfortable showing your work to the world.

Remember to be businesslike in your endeavors. Artists have an undeserved reputation for being somewhat flaky and unreliable, so do all that you can to stave off this impression. Dress professionally when necessary and always behave like a businessperson when dealing with your clients.

Keep trying, and you just might find that your God-given talent is also a Godsend when it comes to making extra money!

Chapter Seven

Cooking Up Dollars— Making Money in the Kitchen

When the weekend rolls around, we all like to indulge a bit, right? What better way to make extra money than to cater to that universal craving for tasty food? Specialty food vendors, bakers, gourmet fruit stands, and many other food-related ideas are solid ways for women entrepreneurs to develop extra income.

Baking to Order

Maia Amos has been baking for years. She even baked her own daughter's wedding cake and has made countless cakes for friends, relatives, and community fund-raisers. And so, after years of giving her talent away, she decided to do it for money! Her business, Mother of the Groom, specializes in baking the "groom's cake," the small extra cake that is traditionally given in small pieces to guests at the end of the reception. "The single girls are supposed to take this small piece of cake and put it under their pillow and then they will dream of their future mate. It's a very old tradition, but not very many caterers and wedding cake shops offer a groom's cake. Right now I am operating on

a pretty small scale, renting space from a friend with a profes-
sional kitchen when I have an order to fill. When the cat dies
I will remodel my kitchen into a certified professional space.
You can't ever have animals around a professional kitchen.
I don't suppose you'd like a cat?" she asked me during our
interview.

Maia has put together a picture portfolio of finished cakes
to show to potential customers and she works at dessert-tasting
fund-raisers and bridal fairs giving away samples of the ornately
frosted dark fruit cake that is traditionally used for a groom's
cake. Her prices vary according to size; a groom's cake that will
serve 60 people would run about $100.

In addition to her groom's cakes, Maia has also advertised
her services to do customized holiday baking. "No one has the
time to do up their Christmas breads and cookies," she says.
"So I step in and bake up whatever they have in mind. That way
they can still impress their friends with little gift bags of home-
baked goodies without the time and effort in the kitchen. Of
course, they never confess that they haven't baked it themselves, so I'm afraid that I don't get any word-of-mouth advertising on this!" Maia is a retired computer programmer who
divides her time between baking and volunteering in the local
Sierra Club gift store. "Compared to computers, baking cakes
is a whole lot more fun!"

Custom Cooking

"I've been making an extra $150 a week for the past ten years,"
says Eleanor Nathan of New York. "After all this time my
clients say they just don't know what they'd do without me!"
Eleanor does what she calls "custom home cooking" for a professional couple, both busy doctors who have neither the time
nor the skill to cook meals at home, but enjoy having home-
cooked meals. That's where Eleanor comes in. She cooks meals
for this busy couple in her own kitchen and delivers food twice
a week to the doctors. The meals are prepared according to the

couple's personal taste and health requirements—only fish and chicken, light on the spices. Eleanor brings two meals on Monday and two meals on Wednesday, and says that she has become "an expert on what freezes well." Her rates are $28 per meal for two, not including the cost of the groceries. And as for training, although Eleanor herself is a graduate of the Cordon Bleu in Paris and has restaurant and catering experience, she believes that what busy couples crave is not fancy food, but good basic meals that any experienced home cook can prepare.

"I only cook for this one couple, sometimes while working full-time at other things. If I had more time and energy I would add more clients. There is a real need for this kind of service in a big-city atmosphere. If you are in the right area you can really do well," says Eleanor. Her advice to new custom cooks looking for clients is to advertise their services at senior citizen condominiums where well-heeled retired people might enjoy having specially cooked meals delivered to them. Hospitals and large office buildings are filled with potential, on-the-go customers who are looking for good food but don't have time to do it themselves. Few people can afford to have a live-in cook or chef, but who wouldn't enjoy a reasonably priced home-cooked meal delivered on a regular basis?

Tom Manning and Nadine Gold cook for more than just one professional couple. Their business, Unique Dining, serves many clients. Both are full-time professional chefs in Orange County, California, who started their own side business in the fall of 1992. For the reasonable price of $260, Tom and Nadine will do the following: customize a menu to suit the client's tastes, do all of the grocery shopping, arrive at the client's home, and, using the client's kitchen, prepare enough food to last two weeks. They will then wrap the meals and mark them clearly, freeze them, and leave the kitchen spotless! Although $260 sounds high, clients are getting ten meals for two people. That breaks down to $13 per person per meal—less than the price of dinner in a modest restaurant.

To find out how to start a business like Tom and Nadine's, call the United States Personal Chef Association (which offers a complete business training system), at (800) 547-7915.

On a much larger scale than Eleanor's individualized cooking or Unique Dining's in-home service are home-cooked meal delivery services that advertise to the general public and may be used on a one-time-only basis. Home on the Range, and Homemade Express are two businesses in California's East Bay Area that mail out a calendar with a month's worth of meals listed. Customers must call and place their order by 2:30 in the afternoon if they want to arrive home from work that evening and find a delicious meal waiting for them on their front porch! Succeeding in a business on this scale is much more difficult, much more costly to undertake, and would only work on a part-time basis for moms at home. A professional kitchen would also be required for a business of this size.

Coffee Delivery Service

I was researching women entrepreneurs in the state of Washington when I discovered Sarah Buck's business card in an Anacortes bookstore. As a confirmed coffee lover, I could immediately see the need for her company, Kaffee Klatsch, a gourmet coffee company that offers home delivery of fresh roasted and specially blended coffees. "My husband is in the military," Sarah explained. "I needed to develop a business that could move across the country if needed, and was not tied down by having a storefront." Motivated by a real love for fresh-roasted coffee, Sarah researched suppliers until she found a solid wholesale contact in San Francisco that offered a superior product for a terrific price. She buys in bulk from her supplier and then repackages the whole beans in smaller quantities for her customers, adding in a 100 percent markup to ensure a tidy profit. "I offer not only convenience for my clients, but also a great product at a great price. Here in Washington, coffee drinkers have become accustomed to the dark, heavy-roasted beans that the Seattle roasters sell. I have educated many of my clients to an appreciation of the lighter, more delicate roasts."

Sarah began by offering her coffee delivery service in residential neighborhoods, delivering on her bicycle, but soon realized that servicing businesses would be another area for potential profits. She has several business customers who order ten pounds a week. In designing her business she followed the traditional model of the old-fashioned neighborhood milkman, establishing weekly or biweekly deliveries to regular customers. Coffee customers pay Sarah by leaving a check in the mailbox or under the mat. During the holidays she adds additional products for her customers, a "Best of the Pacific Northwest" gift basket containing smoked salmon, local jams, and of course, coffee. Despite the popularity of these items, Sarah does not plan to stray from her roots. "I believe that in order to succeed in any business you must have a real love and passion for your product. Many people have gotten into the coffee business because it is popular, not because they love it. I am motivated by a passion for good coffee, and that is what I want to sell." Sarah also tries to share her passion and knowledge with her customers by holding coffee-tasting parties to let them try other types of beans and roasts.

Employed full time in the field of human resources when she founded Kaffee Klatsch, Sarah is now pursuing only her coffee business. It is very possible to run a coffee delivery service on a part-time basis, she believes, depending on how many customers you plan to have. In her early days she went door-to-door, giving out small samples to attract customers, and also spread the word about her service among family and friends. I found her business card on a table in Watermark Books, next to a pot of complimentary coffee that the store provides for customers. Delicious, timely, and rewarding, home coffee delivery can really brew success for a weekend entrepreneur!

Coffee Bean Stand

Another coffee-related, extra-income opportunity is to sell fresh-roasted beans by the pound at farmers' markets. "I've been doing this on the weekend for eight years now," Diane Howe said. "I buy the beans from four different roasters here in town so that I can offer my customers a broad selection."

Weekends at the farmers' market in Roseville, California, are always busy; it's one of the largest and most established in the state and Diane's booth does not come cheap.

Diane bought her business, Coffee and Collectibles, from a friend. "She was only carrying ten types of coffee beans. I now offer my customers over 70 varieties. I also sell coffee filters and small coffee grinders. I've thought about carrying espresso machines or coffee makers, but I think that the price of most equipment is too high for the casual weekend customer stopping by to pick up a pound of beans." A stay-at-home mom during the week, Diane's business has evolved into a simple routine. "Monday morning I phone in orders for more product, the shipment arrives on Thursday, and then I work throughout the day on Saturday and Sunday. What could be simpler?"

Diane has important advice to offer any part-time entrepreneur—take the long view of success. "I see some stand operators counting their till every hour and deciding whether they are a success or not based on what they made that day. You can't approach it like that if you really aim to succeed. You have to look at a year's worth of proceeds to decide what the true picture is." She also recommends against starting a "copy cat" business at a farmers' market. "Your product must be original and of very high quality if you hope to succeed. If you burn a customer with shoddy product once, that's it. They will never forget. I've seen lots of people fail here over the last eight years, and it was because they were trying to fool the public with their product. That never works."

When working a stand at a farmers' market, Diane advises operators to pay attention at all times. "Some people just wander away from their stand in the middle of the day! You have to enjoy people if you want to make this work because you have to be cheerful and attentive all the time. In the summer it gets hot, in the winter it gets cold, but you have to stand there and smile anyway."

Although Diane does not roast the beans herself, there are successful coffee roasters plying their trade at farmers' markets. Coffee roaster Chris Trujillo realized years ago that, while spending the work week as a coffee roaster for a commercial company, he could set up shop with a small electric roaster at outdoor events on the weekend and bring in extra money. "The smell of roasting beans always brings a great crowd," he explained, "and many of those who come to watch end up leaving with a pound or two."

Like wine, coffee is a connoisseur item with many complex elements; in order to sell it effectively you should develop a true appreciation for it. The Specialty Coffee Association of America has educational material available to help businesspeople learn about all aspects of the coffee business. They sponsor an annual conference where informative seminars are held to help you learn more about the coffee business. Here's how you can reach them:

Specialty Coffee Association of America
One World Trade Center, Suite 1200
Long Beach, CA 90831
(310) 983-8090

Espresso Carts

How many coffee-related SAMs can there be? More than you think! All across the country coffee drinkers are reaching for something other than stale canned coffee grounds: fresh roasted and ground coffee has become a national passion. And coffee drinkers don't just want a good cup of coffee at home, the office, or in a restaurant, they want it everywhere! Espresso carts operated by successful weekend entrepreneurs are meeting that need and profiting from it. "I started out with a Nathan's hot dog stand years ago," Mark Sedgley said. "And espresso was one of the extras that I served. I began to notice how popular the espresso was and eventually I decided to phase out the food! It was a great decision." Mark operates his espresso cart at three different farmers' markets throughout the week, selling upwards of 800 cups on a busy day at a dollar apiece!

Espresso carts are expensive. This is not a business with minimum start-up costs. Fancy espresso carts can cost as much as $20,000. Mark suggests looking for a used cart (but check the water lines first to make sure that it is in good condition) or buy one in the state of Washington or Oregon. "Carts are much less expensive there, more like $6,000. The wood's cheaper, I guess." Like the coffee delivery service, operating an espresso cart requires a certain level of expertise. Develop a taste for the perfect cup; the better your product the longer the lines standing in front of your cart at a weekend event! Read books on coffee, talk to experts, and drink, drink, drink, until your espresso palate is developed to the point where you can be certain that your product is of the highest quality.

Mark stresses the importance of location as an element of success. "Don't sign a lease for a location until you know that it will work. I once had a sidewalk corner spot that had incredibly high traffic flowing by, but nobody ever stopped to buy my espresso!" Parks, beaches, art-and-craft fairs, farmers' markets, movie theaters—there are many places that would be ideal spots for a weekend espresso cart. A gas-powered cart is the most mobile and would allow you to move around at will. Don't overlook the fact that a permit is required to operate a sidewalk food stand, however, and first check with local authorities about their requirements before you purchase any equipment. What is legal in one county may well be out of code in another, so be very careful.

Two brothers in Oregon are also catering to the national espresso craving with their stand Dutch Brothers Espresso in Grants Pass, Oregon. Travis and Dane Boersma were in the dairy business but soon realized that the coffee side of "coffee and cream" was a better bet. Their stand is in the corner of a supermarket parking lot and is popular with weekend shoppers.

One reason for the growing popularity of espresso stands is that espresso beverages are difficult for consumers to prepare correctly on their own. The Specialty Coffee Association of America forecasts great growth in the coming years for the cart business and estimates the average yearly gross of a full-time cart at $75,000. Ted Lingle, Executive Director of the

SCAA, has been quoted as saying that "the cost of a coffee cart, which can be as little as $5,000, is a small percentage of the amount of sales it can generate. [And] coffee carts allow retailers the opportunity to physically move their products outside and into a mall, airport, university, or hospital." In addition to offering material on the coffee business, the SCAA also has a free 18-page training brochure on espresso and cappuccino stands.

A Washington-based supplier of espresso carts and related equipment has created a manual to assist entrepreneurs in finding a site for an espresso cart, negotiating a lease, and operating a cart for a profit. Contact Burgess Enterprises for more information (206) 763-0255.

Fresh Juice Bars

Coffee isn't the only thing that Americans are drinking in big gulps. Fresh fruit and vegetable juice is another national craze! As a part of the interest in fitness and health, the "juicing" phenomenon has emerged (also due in large part to late-night infomercials featuring The Juiceman). Fresh juice is good for you, and enthusiasts credit juicing with disease prevention and sometimes even cures. But you won't have to make those kinds of claims with your weekend fresh juice stand; just cater to your clients' taste for delicious fresh juice and squeeze some extra life into your bank account!

Any weekend location that would suit a coffee cart will also suit a fresh juice cart—farmers' markets, country craft fairs, gardening and home shows, or even a busy street corner are ideal spots for a mobile juice bar. A very successful juice stand at one of the busiest California farmers' markets sells only one kind of juice—delicious, homemade lemonade—and the owners have been returning every weekend for years!

Your juice stand should probably offer at least four different varieties of juice. You will need one juicing machine for each type that you offer (juicers require cleaning between flavors, and this slows down production). The most popular juices all feature orange juice as a base. Your customers will flip for delicious juice combos.

To run a successful weekend juice stand you will need the following:

1. A portable cart that meets health department standards. Before you invest any money in a juice cart, check with your local health department to find out what the standards are for your area. Your cart will need to include a power source to run the juicing machines.

2. Several heavy-duty juicers. There are many brands on the market. Choose a model that can withstand frequent use.

3. A wholesale source for your fruit. Produce prices sometimes fluctuate according to the weather (it affects the crop's quality and availability) so you will need to be able to adjust your juice prices to reflect this. You would be wise to link up with a source for organic fruit to offer your customers organic juice.

4. A terrific location. Choose wisely. Your location can mean the difference between astonishing success and expensive failure. Take into account foot traffic, the type of activity in the area, and the typical attendee. The audience for fresh juice is a somewhat upscale one; you will sell more at an organic farmers' market than at a stock-car race.

To learn more about the health properties of juice and to find recipes for crowd-pleasing juices, this book will be of great help:

> *The Complete Book of Juicing*
> Michael T. Murray, N.D.
> Prima Publishing
> $12.95

Have Barbecue, Will Travel

California landscape designer Roy Tatman leads a double life—designing gardens for clients during the week, and then custom barbecuing at garden parties on the weekends! "I used to be in the restaurant business," Roy explained. "But when I made a career change I still had all this cooking stuff lying around. So many friends and former customers loved my cooking that I decided to rent out my barbecue skills on the weekends. You don't need a lot of equipment to do this, some tongs and a flipper, maybe a nice red apron. For most parties I use my own two covered kettle barbecues, but if there will be more than 25 guests I spend $30 and rent a big flat grill. My clients are responsible for providing their own tables, chairs, plates, napkins, drinks, and silverware, I just do the food."

Roy's rates vary according to the menu. "For a basic meal of barbecued steak, beans, and pasta salad I charge $10 a person. It goes up from there depending on how fancy the host wants to get. . . . Appetizer, extra salad offerings, and dessert, well, that will bring the price up considerably." Roy advises other barbecue entrepreneurs to watch their profit margin. It is easy to get carried away and end up losing money on the party.

Although Roy's business is conducted only on the weekends, a certain amount of advance work happens during the week. Picking up groceries and other supplies, prep work on the salads and other dishes, and other small errands should be done before the actual event.

What does it take to start a business like this? Roy recommends it only for folks who have restaurant and cooking experience, and for those who enjoy working with people. "And don't forget to stand upwind and use a long pair of tongs!"

Cookies on the Go

Here is a wacky food-selling idea. "Rick" sells freshly made chocolate chip cookies on the street at a famous farmers' market in Seattle. And I really mean he sells them on the street: from a little red wagon that he pulls down the street. He works no set hours, just bakes up a large batch of cookies whenever he needs a quick cash infusion, dons his tall chef's toque and an attention-getting apron, loads up his little red wagon (decorated with small dolls), attaches a winsomely lettered sign

advertising his wares, and hits the street. His cookies sell for
$1.50 each and they sell quickly!

Now, I'm not sure just how you would go about making a
business like this legal. Certainly you could try it on a slightly
less mobile scale by striking up an arrangement with the owner
of a grocery store or other type of retail establishment. It is, in
essence, selling from a cart. The cart just happens to be a little
red wagon.

Specialty Gourmet Products

The fastest-growing section in grocery stores across the country is the "specialty-gourmet-products" section, filled with
gourmet mustards, sun-dried tomatoes, handmade potato
chips, gourmet cookies, and special sauces. Many of these
products are made by hard-working weekend entrepreneurs
with a favorite family recipe or creation that they have decided
to share with the world. "My wife's grandfather came over
from Cornwall, England, to work in the California gold
mines," Martin Mortenson explained. "His mother handed him
the family's recipe for shortbread cookies before he left
England and told him to fix up a batch whenever he was home-
sick. The recipe was passed down for generations, and always
received rave compliments. "Seven months ago, my wife and I
decided to test-market the cookies to see if they could be sold
commercially, and that's how Grandma Pearlie's Shortbread
was born."

Working with their teenage daughter Shannon, Martin
and his wife Gail found a local baker who was willing to rent
her bakery ovens to them during off hours. "Without her help
we never would have done it. The investment in space and
professional equipment would have been too high," Martin
said. Baking Wednesday evenings and Sunday afternoons, the
Mortensons produce their shortbread cookies in large batches
to satisfy the ever-growing demand on the retail level. Every
month their business has grown in size, but Martin, a full-time

computer salesman, doubts that they will grow Grandma Pearlie's Shortbread into a full-time business. "It is a very labor-intensive business, but since it's the family doing it we save on labor costs. If we had to go out and hire other people to help, it would be a different game entirely." Social Security taxes, worker's compensation, and other time-intensive administrative tasks that arise when employing others, takes more time and money away from a small business like this and quickly eats into the profit. The biggest expense for the Mortensons so far has been a million-dollar liability insurance policy that they took out before they brought their product onto the market. Other large costs include state licensing fees and local business fees. "But we're having fun," Martin adds. "That's the key thing."

Success in the specialty foods market is about the uniqueness and the quality of your product. Once you find a niche to fill, test-market and evaluate the product before you sink large sums of money into it. The Mortensons sent samples to a wide circle of friends and included evaluation postcards to be filled out and returned with honest opinions. Gail Mortenson gave away shortbread samples at a specialty store to test the opinions of total strangers. Attractive and professional-looking packaging for your product is also an important element. A homey touch is sometimes nice, but customers in gourmet shops are looking for a certain amount of sophistication in the look of their food.

It is possible for a part-time specialty food product entrepreneur to handle local distribution of her product on her own, but to expand state or nationwide, professional distributors must be found. Ask the merchandise buyers at local gourmet food stores for the names of specialty product distributors. A distributor will charge a percentage of your sales, but the increased business should make it worthwhile.

Karen Jackson of Karen's Mustard had another suggestion. "Another way to handle distribution is to go to the food shows and find other small businesses with gourmet products who might form a distribution network with you. They could also sell your product in their area, while you distribute their product along with yours in your area. It is a good way to increase your effectiveness."

Karen went into business selling mustard made from a recipe that her dad, Herb Jackson, created. She warns that anyone going into this type of business will need to have some free time available during the week to make sales calls with merchandise buyers who simply aren't available on the weekends. A gourmet food producer's weekends are spent either demonstrating her product in stores that carry it (giving away samples to customers) or selling her product at retail price direct to the public at craft fairs or farmers' markets.

There are several levels of seriousness in the specialty food market. On a smaller scale than either the Mortensons' shortbread or Karen's mustard, Pat, a school secretary, makes and sells her own specially created Champagne jelly at Christmas bazaars and to her colleagues at school during the holiday season. "I noticed that lots of people bring things to school to sell, so I decided that I would too. For years I'd been making a recipe for Champagne jelly that I had created by combining two other recipes. Everyone seemed to like it so I realized that I already had a popular product on my hands. Every December I take special orders and also make up enough to sell at two or three craft boutiques. Over the course of the season I make enough money to buy all of my Christmas gifts! It's been a big help to my budget."

One of the attractive features of developing and marketing a specialty gourmet food product is the high price tag attached to it! Customers who shop at gourmet food stores are not looking for bargains, but are shopping for unique, unusual, and delicious treats, and they are very willing to pay more for them. Start rummaging through your mother's old recipe card file. Perhaps there is a secret recipe in your family that can cook up a profit for you!

To learn more about what types of products are already on the market and what seems to be missing from the market, an industry magazine is a good source of information. *Fancy Food* is the magazine to read; call Talcott Publishing at (312) 664-4040 for subscription information. Once you decide to learn more, you should attend one of the gourmet products shows that are held several times a year around the country. For more information, call the show's producer, the National Association for the Specialty Food Trade, (212) 482-6440.

According to the NASFT, the specialty food industry is growing and thriving. A recent survey revealed that consumers short on large sums of disposable income are "finding more gratification in pasta than Porsches." So now is definitely the time to get revved up and start selling your own specialty product!

Thinking It Through

Food preparation is a tricky field, and a much-regulated one. Whenever food that will be consumed by the public is involved, each individual county, city, and state gets in on the act. You must investigate the regulations in your area before starting up any food-related venture. In addition to health regulations you will have to take into consideration the following:

1. Licenses—Once you meet the regulations and standards in your area you will be able to get a license. Needless to say, there are fees involved.

2. Product liability—"Why take chances?" advises Martin Mortenson of Grandma Pearlie's Shortbread. In this litigious society it is wise to be protected against the possibility of a lawsuit. Speak to your insurance broker about liability insurance.

3. Custom kitchens—Building a kitchen that meets the health standards is not an inexpensive undertaking. It is possible to rent space in a custom kitchen to get started. Check for ads in local newspapers and magazines that cater to "foodies." Many churches have professional kitchens. You might start on a small scale by checking to see if you can rent time in a church kitchen.

4. Taste and quality—These are two factors that you must not skimp on if you plan to become a success in the food business. Invest a great deal of time and patience in developing your product so that what you take to market is of the highest quality and the best possible taste. Fancy packaging may sell your product once, but taste and quality will keep your customers coming back.

5. Expenses and start-up costs—Starting a specialty food business from scratch is not cheap; neither is buying an espresso cart or other weekend food stand. Before you launch yourself into the wonderful world of food, please consider how much it will cost to get started, and how long it will take before you can realistically expect to see a return on your investment. If you need fast money, the food business is not for you.

In lieu of a fancy (and expensive) professional kitchen, you can also hire a "co-producer" to produce your product for you. These are food development and production companies who can produce your mustard, honey spread, marmalade, or other specialty product in large quantities at wholesale prices; the minimum run is generally 250 cases of product. To find a co-producer in your area, you can ask other small-time specialty food entrepreneurs, or look for advertisements in professional food magazines.

In the gourmet food business, as in other types of businesses, it is important to keep on eye on trends. If you don't already have an idea for a gourmet food product, why don't you brainstorm on some of these current trends:

- Meatless eating—Everyone is eating less red meat nowadays. Why not develop a weekend food stand that caters to this desire?

- Lowfat foods—Along with less red meat, we are also working hard to lower fat intake. Many favorite foods like muffins are now showing up in fat-reduced or fat-free versions. What can you develop in a fat-free way?

- Gourmet teas—Coffee is already hot, but gourmet tea is not far behind! Check out the new teas from Republic of Tea (the brainchild of the folks who developed Banana Republic) and Royal Tea. These entrepreneurs are at the forefront of a growing interest in very expensive upscale imported teas. There is a way for weekend entrepreneurs to cash in, perhaps a tea stand or a tea-tasting club? Think about it.

- International food—Thai, Indian, Caribbean—our taste buds are going international and there is still plenty of room for entrepreneurs to develop international food stands, spice and flavoring packages, sauces, and specialty cookbooks.

Gourmet foods and food-related products can be a terrifically profitable and fun business. So roll up your sleeves, go in your kitchen, and get creative! Who knows where it will lead.

Chapter Eight

Long Shots—
Great Ideas for
Special People

Here are some terrific ideas that won't work for just anyone, anywhere. These ideas require special talents (like writing and publishing), special locations (tourist areas), or special knowledge (books and literature). But each of these business ideas is a real extra cash bonanza if you have the special ingredients to make it work!

Big-Time Profits from Small-Time Publishing

I have been working in the world of books for some dozen-odd years now, and I have had the chance to observe many different styles and types of publishing. As I mentioned in the beginning pages of this book, since 1989 I have been self-publishing a small booklet that I wrote about an inexpensive way to travel. Over the years I have sold several thousand copies of my book, *The Air Courier's Handbook*. At 44 pages, the book is far too small to be carried in bookstores and my only sales outlet has been mail order. Glamorous as the prospect of being published by a big publishing house may seem to an author, I must say that my "small-time" publishing project is far more personally profitable than most standard publishing arrangements. Not only is it unusually profitable, it was not at all hard to do! Read on, and I will show you how anyone with writing skills can find a successful topic, publish a booklet, and market it for an impressive extra-income opportunity.

Several years ago my friend Sherry Miller moved to Indonesia, a very expensive plane ride away from my home base of Northern California. In college I had heard that traveling as an air courier was a cheap way to fly, so I set about to investigate. My big break came the night I overheard a conversation in a restaurant about air courier travel and boldly interrupted to learn more. And what I learned was valuable indeed, so valuable that I took all of my new information, did some more research, and wrote a short book about air courier travel that fills a gaping information hole for budget-minded travelers.

My original plan was to write a book of 75 to 80 pages, hire a designer to achieve the right "look," and send it off to a short-run printer for a run of two or three thousand perfect-bound books. After all, I was a book publishing professional and had my reputation to think of! During the time that I was working on my manuscript I attended a writer's conference in the seaside town of Carmel. I spent the lunch hour sitting across from a woman who had written a booklet about hydroponic farming that she was successfully marketing through small ads in the back of magazines like *Mother Jones* and *Whole Earth*. Her booklet was a basic 12-page, photocopied and stapled piece of work, and she was anxious for my professional editorial opinion. I held her booklet in my hands, opened my mouth to speak, and promptly shut it. In seconds I had been struck by an incredible revelation.

I had been on the verge of suggesting that she upgrade the appearance of her work, spend a bit more money on design and production to achieve a more professional look. And the thunderbolt idea that struck me mute was this—excessive money spent on design and production for a mail-order book was a waste of money. Readers of her ad in *Mother Jones* were strictly interested in her *information,* the only thing that they were seeking. Information, pure and simple, instead of a fancy book to put on a shelf. Books produced for the mail-order market need to be heavy on information but not necessarily professionally produced. Your customers will be very happy with the information, and you will be pleased by improved profits!

Using this new discovery I started rethinking my air courier book. I scaled down my original plan for the length, dropped all plans to hire a designer, and tossed the short-run printers' brochures in the trash. After several weeks of work this is what I produced: *The Air Courier's Handbook: Travel the World on a Shoestring* by Jennifer Basye. A 44-page stapled booklet filled with all the knowledge you need to travel as an air courier, as well as phone numbers of air courier companies and their flight destinations. It was decorated with cartoons and illustrations by my brother, Paul Basye, with a cover design using uncopyrighted clip-art. This booklet costs a little over $1 to produce; I sell it through the mail for $10. Instead of printing up 2,000 copies right away, I go to the local copy shop and have the book made up in batches of 250 at a time, greatly reducing the money I have tied up in inventory. After subtracting for the cost of an envelope and postage, I make somewhere in the neighborhood of $8 profit for every book sold. With the extra money that I have made from this book I have taken two trips to Asia— trips that I could not otherwise afford. Naturally I flew as an air courier!

How can you do this too? With careful planning it is possible for anyone with average writing skills to create a booklet that will sell well through mail order. Finding a valuable topic that will produce sales is the first step. Saving money and making money are far and away the two best topics for a mail-order booklet that works; food and recipe books are also popular. Every day you come across small pieces of information that, properly packaged, could form the basis for a good booklet. Look carefully at your life—what (or who) do you know? Do you have a time- or money-saving trick that would save hours or dollars each week? Millions of people buy books of housecleaning tips, just ask author Don Aslett. As a mother have you learned endless ways to keep small children occupied and quiet hour after hour? Just think how many harried mothers would love to know your secret. Has your recipe for caramel fudge been sought after by friends and relatives? Page after page of small classified ads for recipes appear each week in the *National Enquirer,* so someone must be buying them! Good ideas are all around and could pop into your mind at any time. While working on the *Foraging* section in Chapter 3, I realized that there is an opportunity for a booklet, *Secrets of a Successful Forager*, or *Money on the Forest Floor,* something along those lines. Keep your eyes and ears open for ideas at all times. If you know how to research a topic, you can write about anything—what about a small travel booklet that lists hotels in Europe that offer discounts for senior citizens? Think of the size of the potential market for that one!

To get your creative juices flowing and help you discover an idea that will work for you, sit down with a blank piece of paper and begin to brainstorm with these terms:

101 Ways to . . .	A Parent's Guide to . . .
An Artist's Guide to . . .	A Hiker's Guide to . . .
Time-Saving Tips on . . .	The Money-Saving Guide to . . .
Never Spend Money	The Complete Traveler's
Again on . . .	Guide to . . .
The Beachlover's Guide to . . .	The Insider's Guide to . . .
A Woman's Guide to . . .	The Retiree's Handy Guide to . . .
Love Secrets of . . .	The Romantic's Guide to . . .

Well, you get the idea. The possibilities are endless. Once you arrive at an idea, make sure that the topic you choose meets these criteria:

1. Large potential audience—How many people would be interested in this book? Can my target group (parents, nurses, pilots, whoever) afford to buy a booklet?

2. Compelling topic—What is it about this book that will inspire my target audience to buy it? Will they save money, time, or really learn something that can improve their lives?

3. "Researchable" topic—Do I know enough already, or can I research this topic thoroughly and really deliver what I promise in the title?

4. Targeted media—Is there a good way to reach my target audience? What newspapers and magazines might they read? Will these papers review or write about my booklet?

If you can answer "yes" to all of these questions, the topic you have chosen has a good chance of succeeding as a mail-order book or booklet. The next step, of course, is to research and write the book! Don't make the book longer than it has to be (you will waste money), but don't cheat your readers. Deliver what you promise and more.

In years past the cost of producing a professional-looking book or booklet was prohibitive, but with the ever-increasing availability of desktop publishing software it is now possible for you to create a quality product on your own. Many copy shops and desktop publishing stores allow you to rent their equipment on an hourly basis and work on your project at their facility. The store employees can help you learn your way around a desktop publishing program, and there are several good books that teach the skills you need. In a matter of hours you can produce a great-looking book that will present your information in a clear, readable, and easily accessible style. Don't get too carried away on the design, and when it comes time to print up copies of your book, start by printing small numbers.

Now on to the next step—selling that book! If you have chosen your topic wisely by concentrating on a compelling topic with a large and affluent potential audience who reads newspapers and magazines, marketing and selling your book should be easy. Let's study the example of *The Air Courier's Handbook.* Targeted to adventurous world travelers looking for an inexpensive way to travel, my first sales method was to place ads in small off-beat travel magazines like *Great Expeditions* or *International Travel News.* The cost of advertising was inexpensive and I was assured that I was sending my message out to the right group of potential customers. Each one of these ads was a modest success; in each instance I made twice as much money in book sales as I'd spent on the cost of the ad. I did this for the first year and sold several hundred copies this way. In my second year of business I had grown more comfortable with my product (I kept expecting people to complain about the size; instead I got fan mail on what a great source of hard-to-find info it was!) and more confident about my knowledge of the topic. I wrote up a press release about *The Air Courier's Handbook* and sent several dozen press releases and sample books off to travel editors at newspapers and magazines around the country. The reaction was incredible! Over the course of a year I received several big write-ups in the travel sections of major newspapers like the *Boston Globe* and the *San Francisco Chronicle* and orders just poured in. There was one heady period of time when I would find thirty or more book orders a day in my post office box, $300 a day in extra income. Unfortunately that only lasted for a few weeks, but since then stories have appeared regularly about my little book (I update the book every year and send press releases and sample books out every time) and I average between 10 and 15 orders a week. My costs for this publicity campaign were limited to postage and the hard cost of the book (around $1 each) and the rewards have been extraordinary. Free publicity is much, much more effective than paid advertising. At every step of the way as you produce your booklet you should not only be considering the needs and expectations of your customers, but also consider how the media will view your book. If you send out a professional product that is newsworthy, you can get publicity. If you send out a shoddy little book on a topic of no interest, an editor will pitch it in the trash.

Self-publishing is a very rewarding experience, emotionally and financially. Choose your topic wisely, produce a good product, and enjoy the fruits of your labor. My business address is listed below, and I would be happy to give you my opinion on your booklet idea. Send me a letter about your project and I will respond with my honest reaction about its potential success. If you would like to see an example of "small-time publishing," send $5 and I will send you a copy of *The Air Courier's Handbook* at half price. You can reach me by writing to Big City Books, 7047 Hidden Lane, Loomis, CA, 95650. Happy publishing!

To learn more about how to put together a book like this, I recommend:

Publishing Short-Run Books:
How to Paste Up and Reproduce Books
Instantly Using Your Quick-Print Shop
Dan Poynter
Para Publications
$5.95

Bike Rentals

What better way for tourists to spend a beautiful day on the coast than biking slowly along a scenic road until the sun sets, stopping whenever they'd like to take in the view and have an impromptu picnic. . . . Unless they packed their bikes in with their luggage, this is only a dream. Only a dream until you open up a weekend bike rental business, that is!

Domestic tourism is up in all areas of the country, and many new tourist destinations are emerging. If you were far-sighted enough to settle in one of these places, or if there is not already a bike rental business in your tourist town, get busy and start one. Every weekend you could be making money while happy tourists pedal around on your bikes taking in the sights.

It is not necessary to have expensive equipment or a fancy location to start this business. Unless the terrain of your town requires mountain bikes to get around, you are better off buying old balloon tire route bikes, basic one- or two-speed models from the '60s, and simple children's bikes to use as rentals. Paint them all a highly identifiable color, make sure the tires and the brakes are in good condition, buy simple bicycle locks for the customers to use for the afternoon, and you are set.

You will not need a fancy storefront for your business; the side parking lot of another business will do just fine. Make sure that you are located on the most popular street in town, preferably one with high foot traffic. Approach the owners of a shop that you think is well situated and ask if you can rent a corner of their parking lot on the weekends. You only need enough space to set up a few bike stands and a sandwich board or sign to advertise your rental service. What could be simpler?

In addition to attracting rental customers from foot traffic, approach local hotels and bed-and-breakfasts to let them know bike rentals are available. They could steer customers your way and might be interested enough to rent a few bikes from you on the weekends for guests to use. Printing up a simple brochure or flyer to stock in the lobbies is a wise move; also, alert the local tourist board to your new business.

If you care to take this one step further you could develop bicycle tours of your area. Read the "Odds and Ends" chapter for information about designing and leading custom tours. Another related (although more complicated) idea is to develop a bicycle pedicab service in your tourist town. Not recommended for hilly areas, this is a popular service in the Southern California town of Westwood and in several other tourist towns.

Book Scout

"There are some book scouts who stop by every two weeks with eight big boxes of books and leave with around $500," used bookstore employee Gina Lewis told me. "Once I developed an understanding of the business I started to do it too. Walking home from a friend's house one day I stopped by a garage sale, spent $8.50 and later that afternoon made $37 by selling those same books at a used bookstore." Not bad for an afternoon stroll, and a fine way for book lovers to make a little extra money on the weekends.

Not every book can be resold to a used bookstore for profit. Before you rush out to hit every garage and yard sale you can find, familiarize yourself first with what types of books your local used bookstores are interested in. Some used bookstores specialize in metaphysical books, or collectible cookbooks, or travel literature; others stock general interest titles. Chances are that there are several used bookstores in your area, each with its own personality and specialized need. "The best way to learn is just by doing it," Gina advises. "And you will learn a lot from the buyer in the bookstore. As they go through the books that you have brought in they will probably explain why they won't take this book or that book, explaining that this one is too old, and they already have several copies of that one. . . ."

To give you a basic understanding of the kinds of books that you should keep an eye out for at flea markets or garage and yard sales, here is a brief list of valuable categories of books:

- Hardcover cookbooks—The newer, the better, but there is a market for older titles as well.

- Classic children's books—Hardcover, illustrated books are the most valuable for collectors, but are the most difficult to find on a garage sale table.

- Current hardcover fiction—The new Danielle Steel? Sure, pay a quarter for it and you might be able to sell it to a used bookstore for up to 30 percent of the list price.

- Hardcover horror and fantasy fiction—There are book scouts out there who can now send their children to college on the money they have made from early first-edition Stephen King novels. I know a policeman who supplements his income with collectible horror books; he also suggests watching for books by Clive Barker and Dean Koontz.

- Antique and collectible historical books—There is a steady market for early California books, as well as old books about most states and regions. In California the most collectible books are those on the "Zamarano Eighty." Uncovering one of these books at an estate sale will reap large rewards.

- Early metaphysical and occult works—Books by Edgar Cayce and Aleister Crowley and books on astrology, the Tao, and any other type of metaphysical book are very collectible.

- Trade paperback literature—Trade paperbacks are paperback books that are somewhat larger than mass-market pocket paperbacks. Works of fiction in this size can easily be resold to used bookstores. Don't pay more than 25¢ apiece at a garage sale, and you may triple your money at the used bookstore.

- First edition fiction—older works by Fitzgerald, Faulkner, and Hemingway are valuable, and so are newer works of fiction. In Chicago, for instance, first editions of mystery writer Sara Paretsky fetch very high prices. Keep your eyes open and you will discover amazing prices! I once bought a first-edition Hemingway in very fine condition for $75.

Once you get in the habit of scouting for collectible books you will be hooked. As a confirmed book lover, I search constantly for books to keep (I kept the Hemingway) and sell. A related way to make extra money with used books is to buy leather-bound books to resell to interior decorators. Believe it or not, there are folks out there who want a shelf full of impressive leather-bound books that are part of the decorating scheme! Talk to interior decorators to see if there is a market for "books-by-the-yard" in your area before you get started.

Niche Newsletters

Another potential publishing moneymaker is found in the burgeoning field of niche newsletters. Once seldom seen, newsletters are cropping up all over to serve all types of topics. If you read the section on *Herb Farming* in Chapter 3 you know about the newsletter that goes out to folks who grow herbs for profit; there are also newsletters for diverse groups such as emergency room nurses, retired firefighters, and snowboarders.

Lynda Blankenship found an unserved niche when she started her newsletter *Lynda's Monthly Update* for avid collectors of Dickens Village lighted Christmas houses made by Department 56. What started as a casual letter to other collectors about Department 56 turned into a profitable newsletter filled with news about upcoming products, current prices, and availability of pieces, along with a profitable section of the newsletter that serves as a clearinghouse for collectors buying, selling, and trading among themselves. What better way to enjoy your own hobby than to find a way to profit from it?

Newsletters targeted to small audience niches should be well-designed and readable, but needn't be extravagantly designed and overly colorful. Many beginning publishers get sidetracked into trying to produce a fancy newsletter when a modest one will do. *Book Bound* is eight pages, two legal-sized pieces of recycled paper folded in half. "We tried to give it a literary look," says James Meek about his newsletter for literary folk. "We didn't start with much money and we tried hard to keep our costs low by making an attractive but simple newsletter."

A different type of newsletter is produced in Allston, Massachusetts, by Steve Lantos. His monthly newsletter, *Travel Unlimited,* serves to keep air couriers informed with up-to-the-minute intelligence on prices of courier flights and other cheap air travel around the world. Because I only update my book *The Air Courier's Handbook* (see *Big-Time Profits from Small-Time Publishing* in this chapter) once a year; I subscribe to Steve's newsletter to keep abreast of courier trends.

At $25 a year, Steve has subscribers scattered around the world. Unlike the typeset and designed give-away newsletter *Book Bound, Travel Unlimited* is produced by Steve himself on a typewriter. Each issue consists of two pages of typed information copied and stapled together. No advertising is included, just good solid information. Not the most elegant newsletter, but the information itself is so valuable to his readers that no one has ever complained!

Sometimes a small newsletter will hit it big. That's what happened to Amy Dacyczyn and her newsletter *The Tightwad Gazette.* Amy started her newsletter as a way to spread the word about living a cheapskate life (reusing vacuum cleaner bags, making soap last longer, and buying oats for baking from animal feed stores!), the media picked up on it and she has now hit it big with both her newsletter and a best-selling book based on her ideas. You never know where your small newsletter might lead you!

What kind of a newsletter does the world need? Flip back to the section on "Big-Time Profits from Small-Time Publishing;" many of the same standards and criteria that a booklet needs to meet also apply to a niche newsletter. How large an audience exists? Is this audience already served by a newsletter or magazine? Can you do a better job? Become a keen observer of the world and its trends and you will develop a knack for spotting a potential audience that could use a newsletter. Some hard-working entrepreneurs in Oakland have started a newsletter for Karaoke lovers! In the "Cooking for Dollars" chapter 1 talk about the tremendous interest in gourmet coffees, and the growing interest in gourmet teas. There is a hole in the market for newsletters that cater to coffee and tea lovers. Travel articles about coffee plantations in exotic places, tasting comparisons, recommendations, recipes, and more could be covered in a newsletter for this audience. Get started now and be sure to send me a copy when you are finished!

Three resource books that will help you get started are:

Newsletter Sourcebook
Mark Beach
North Light Books
$26.95

Publishing Newsletters
Howard Penn Hudson
Simon and Schuster
$13.95

Publish Magazines and Newspapers
with a Macintosh Computer
Harris Smith
Upper River Press
$16.95

Used Jeans, Vintage, and Collectible Clothing

"It's a fashion thing," says Jim Goodykoontz, when I asked him to explain the craze for used jeans and collectible clothing. "Japan and Europe and other places, they know more about Levi-Strauss than most Americans do. Purely American stuff, they just go crazy for it." Jim started to develop an interest in vintage clothing while working as a Park Ranger in California. "I got transferred to the Governor's Mansion museum in Sacramento, and I found out that if I dressed in vintage clothing I could get out of wearing the standard issue ranger's uniform. So I started to look around at what was available." He started out looking for turn-of-the-century men's clothing and slowly his collection grew to include all manner of vintage clothing. Jim also began to notice how much vintage clothing dealers would pay for the things he found, and a SAM was quickly developed!

The big craze nowadays is for used jeans. The jeans are sent overseas to be sold for much higher prices than they fetch here in America. Not just used Levi's, but also old Lee and Wrangler jeans are worth money to a used jeans dealer. "There is a ready market for used 501s. They sell for anywhere between $35 and $60 out of the country, and there are dealers all over who are combing the countryside looking for jeans to buy. Most big cities are pretty much glutted, but small towns and out-of-the-way spots should be a great place to go looking," Jim suggested. "By getting up early to hit the garage sales, it is still possible for an energetic person to make anywhere from $300 to $800 a month with used jeans."

The overseas market is crazy for other vintage American clothing as well; keep your eyes open for any of the following items:

- old leather motorcycle jackets
- WWII leather bomber jackets
- Air Force or Army nylon bomber jackets
- old Hawaiian shirts ('40s and '50s)
- vintage bowling shirts
- old fancy western clothing
- vintage men's formal wear
- any fancy men's stuff from the '50s (Jim described it as "the kind of stuff Ricky Ricardo would wear")

Clothing from the '70s is pretty hot right now, so you might also start keeping an eye out for platform shoes and wide bell bottoms. And if you are successful in finding any of these items, what do you do? Why, call Jim Goodykoontz, of course.

"I'd love to buy stuff from people all across the country. California is getting pretty tapped out, but I know that there are closets all across America that contain valuable things." Call Jim at (916) 442-5342 and tell him what you've found. But remember, you've got to get up pretty early to hit those garage sales before your competitors do!

Worm Farming

Throughout history, wonderful things have been said about the lowly worm. Cleopatra called the worm "a sacred animal," Aristotle said that worms were the "guts of the soil," and Darwin himself said that they are "more powerful than the African elephant and more important to the economy than the cow." As it turns out, worms are also a way to earn some extra money!

Cindy Nelson is the owner of City Worms & Compost in San Francisco. She does a brisk business selling wooden worm boxes for composting food waste to home recyclers. "Well, I make and sell worm boxes large enough to handle the garbage of one person, two people, or four people. You feed them your food waste, you see, and they eat it and in turn make a wonderfully fine soil that you can use in your garden." Cindy's wooden worm boxes are not cheap. She builds them out of exterior-grade plywood and her customers pay from $45 for the one-person box to $110 for the four-person box. And that does not include the worms.

Red worms are the key element. Red worms are voracious eaters of waste. One pound of worms will eat one-half pound of food waste a day. With the spotlight on landfills and garbage nowadays, many cities across the country are mandating that waste be reduced, and worms are a trendy way to do this. "This is definitely a growth area for entrepreneurs," Cindy advises. "Building and selling worm boxes is ideal for part-time income." Cindy alerted many environmental, composting, and recycling groups about her worm boxes and these groups do much of her publicity for her. They pass out her brochures, recommend her service, and steer customers her way.

She originally planned to only build boxes, but the red worms themselves have been in such demand that Cindy has also started a small worm farm in her backyard. "I have two raised beds of 10-inch rows, and I feed the worms manure. I sell worms for $12 a pound (subtract the weight of the earth!), and then if my customer wants me to set up the worm box I will do it for a $15 set-up fee. I coat the inside of the worm box with vegetable oil and add a layer of shredded newspaper and just a handful of soil. Once the worms start eating garbage they produce 'castings,' which is very enriched soil. Lots of my customers put the worm box under the sink and feed the worms there, but others put it out in the yard. The boxes have hinged lids and are pretty sturdy. You could use it for a bench if you wanted to."

Cindy learned about worms and worm boxes by attending a master composter training program offered in her area. She suggests contacting the local office in your area that deals with recycling, garbage, or waste removal to inquire about composting classes. Gardening groups might also teach worm composting. She recommends a book to help beginners understand more about worms and how to learn to build the boxes:

Worms Eat My Garbage
Mary Appelhoff
Flowerfield Enterprises
10332 Shaver Rd.
Kalamazoo, MI 49002
$10.95

"Real People" Modeling and Movie Extra Work

Don't have a willowy-thin body and movie star looks? That doesn't necessarily disqualify you from working as a print model or an on-screen extra. There is always a need for "real" people to star in or be in the background of a shot to give it an authentic look. Yes, this is certainly a "long-shot" way to make money, but don't just dismiss it out of hand. First open your phone book to "Casting" and see if there is a company in your area that specializes in casting commercials. If there is, pick up the phone and call them! You will need to have professional photographs done for them to keep on file. A word of warning: You should not have to pay any kind of "fee" to a casting agency, nor should you have to pay money to attend any special kind of course. The modeling business is rife with rip-offs, so watch out.

The movie business also needs "real people" to be in the background of shots. Ordinary-looking folks to walk down the street behind the camera, sit at a lunch counter, or otherwise add an authentic air to what is going on. Sometimes hundreds of extras are hired for a movie, either for the day or sometimes for weeks on end, at a going rate of $100 a day.

How can you connect with the companies that hire movie extras? Call your area's Chamber of Commerce and find out if they have a film commission. As expenses have risen in the Los Angeles and New York areas, many film companies have found that it is much less costly to film in small-town America, and many Chambers of Commerce have found it is worth their while to let film companies know about their areas, The Chamber of Commerce Film Commission should be aware of any films that are currently scheduled to be filmed in your area and could put you in touch with the folks in charge. Take a chance and check into this; you could see yourself up on the silver screen someday! I will repeat the same stern warning about movie casting as I mentioned about modeling: Don't pay anyone a "fee," and don't sign up to take an expensive course.

House Modeling

Kind of an odd way to describe it, but the same folks who need real-looking people need real-looking houses for commercials. My own mother has made fine money ($150 an hour!) on more than one occasion when her house was used as a backdrop for a national car ad. To find out about "location scouts" operating in your area and how to contact them, contact the film commission at your local Chamber of Commerce.

Cigar Concession

After languishing for many years as a rich man's accessory, cigars and cigar smoking are suddenly "hot." The popularity of cigar smoking has grown steadily for the last five years and has achieved widespread acceptance, even among women! Cigar stores are popping up in even the smallest towns, and it is a rare magazine that doesn't occasionally feature a photo of a celebrity posing with a cigar.

How can you make cigar smoking work for you? I discovered a very clever extra-income business at the bar of an Italian restaurant in Southern California. A very beautiful wooden humidor (a special box that keeps cigars at the proper temperature) filled with high-end cigars was sitting on the bar and when I inquired about the price of a particular cigar (yes, I am one of those women) the bartender replied, "I'll have to look it up. That humidor doesn't belong to us, a local woman keeps it stocked." I had stumbled upon a very trendy SAM, sitting right in front of me! I spoke to the restaurant manager about how it worked.

"She comes by every few days to check on the stock and keep it well supplied. Our bar customers pay cash for the cigars and we keep a percentage and hand over the rest to her."

This enterprising woman had put together a fancy binder filled with descriptions of the cigars, their ratings from a popular cigar magazine, and their prices. Once she convinced the restaurant owners that this would be a good way for them to add to their nightly profit, it was a great low-maintenance business.

You will, however, have to find a source of wholesale cigars. Start by making the acquaintance of your local cigar retailer and see how much you can learn about local suppliers.

Accessories are also starting to appear in and around the cigar craze. Creative thinkers might be able to spot other ways to profit from the new interest in cigars by designing T-shirts for cigar lovers, jewelry, smoking jackets, or even custom ashtrays. In the same way that a craze like snowboarding spawned special shirts, hats, and other accessories around it, so will cigars. Keep your eyes (and your mind) open!

Thinking It Through

What's to think through? You pretty much have to wing it on these ideas because they all require special components—talent, creativity, imagination, guts, knowledge, wackiness, location, and stick-to-it-iveness. Chances are that if you are missing just one of these ingredients, the idea will not work. Please be clear-eyed in your self-assessment before you launch yourself into one of these long shots. The pay-offs are terrific, but failure is no fun for anyone.

This is my favorite chapter. Our country was built by people willing to take a long shot on a crazy idea—an idea about harnessing electricity, about developing a telephone, about building a personal computer. I certainly don't count myself among these lofty inventors, but I do believe that anyone who tries out an unusual idea and tries to make it work has a right to be proud. Don't let your friends, family, or spouse try to make you feel silly when you turn on your computer to compose the first issue of your niche newsletter. Ignore your family's snickers as you wake up early every Saturday morning to go off to neighborhood yard sales in search of used blue jeans and collectible books. Hold your head high, and be proud that you are taking a chance in life instead of sitting around complaining about how much better things could be!

Chapter Nine

Moms at Home—Extra Money for Entrepreneurial Mothers

We all know how much work stay-at-home moms do, day in and day out, but the darned shame of it is no one pays us! But for the many moms who would like to save up an extra nest egg or contribute to the household income, there are countless ways to stay at home with the kids and make money while you are there! Many of the women I interviewed for this book are full-time moms who have discovered truly inventive ways to make extra cash. I made it a point to ask each of them which business ideas in this book were best suited to moms at home, and this chapter lists the top suggestions from these entrepreneurial experts! The ideas presented here are in capsule form. For the full description of each business and how to succeed in it, please turn to the complete listings in Chapters 1 through 8.

Top Ten Weekend Businesses for Moms

1. Herb Farming—Herbs are big business, and getting bigger all the time. Tending an herb garden in your backyard is an ideal pursuit for a full-time mom. The garden and its plants can be cared for throughout the week as a part of your at-home routine. Deliveries to accounts

can be managed while kids are in school, or the kids can even ride along and learn about the business at your side! If you run a stand at a farmers' market on the weekends, the kids can easily come along for a morning (the markets seldom last all day) or spend a day hanging out with Dad. You can find a more complete description and sources of information on herb farming on page 52.

2. Cut Flower Business—Much like herb farming, growing and selling cut flowers is perfect for moms. Perhaps you could even combine the two pursuits and sell upscale bouquets that mix herbs and flowers. What a wonderfully rewarding way to spend time at home, taking care of your children and your beautiful flower garden at the same time, knowing that both children and flowers will reward you hundreds of times over. The fresh flower business is fully detailed on page 42.

3. Hand-Rolled Beeswax Candles—This is my favorite money-making craft, and I do it to great success on the weekends. You can roll candles late into the night when your children are sleeping; each candle takes only seconds to make and sells for a terrific profit. And you get the added bonus of a pleasant beeswax smell pervading the room while you work. Schools and day-care centers are a steady source of craft fairs, so you may find that it is not hard at all to find opportunities to sell your wares to friends and fellow moms. You also get to decorate your own home inexpensively with very posh-looking beeswax candles. Look in Chapter 4 for the run-down on this business idea, page 75.

4. Antiques and Collectibles Dealer—Most antique galleries require very little in the way of actual hours; maintaining a small space in a cooperative gallery might require you to be there as few as four hours a month. The rest of the time you can scout out estate sales, flea markets, and yard sales looking for bargain wares to resell in your space. Find out more about this rewarding business idea in the "Old-Fashioned Money" chapter, page 34.

5. Christmas Bazaars and Open House Craft Boutiques—A terrific way to earn extra money around the holidays, organizing Christmas bazaars and craft boutiques is also an awful lot of fun. Much of your organizing can be done while the children are at school or asleep, so full-time moms find that this works well with their other commitments. Once you successfully stage a Christmas bazaar you might be hooked on the idea of being a weekend entrepreneur and venture into a year-round business. See page 38.

6. Foraging the Wild for Profit—Foraging in the wild for supplies to use in craft projects or for wild items to market is a terrific enterprise

for the whole family! You can turn an afternoon's outing into a geology lesson, history lesson, or nature hike while at the same time picking up things that will turn into cash later on. Read more about foraging in the "Old-Fashioned Money" chapter, page 45. This might be right for you and your family.

7. Niche Newsletter—Housewife Amy Dacyczyn made the decision to stay home with her children and earn extra money by publishing *The Tightwad Gazette*. With national exposure for her newsletter and a best-selling book, she has exceeded her wildest dreams. Small newsletters are cropping up to serve the interest of many different groups, from snowboarders to fans of sing-along karaoke bars. Find the right targeted audience for which to publish, and your niche newsletter could bring money in the mail every day! Learn more about newsletter publishing in the "Long Shots" chapter, page 158.

8. Custom Window Coverings with Matching Bedspreads—With a flair for design and a skill for sewing, you can cash in on the craze for custom window treatments. Sew window coverings from beautiful fabrics your customers have purchased and make matching bedspreads while working at your own pace in an extra room in your house. There is also a large demand for custom curtains and bedspreads for nurseries and children's rooms. The "Crafty Business" chapter has a complete description of this business on page 72.

9. Potpourri and Herbal Products—What better way to enjoy your own beautiful garden than to fill it with roses, lavender, and culinary herbs to turn into high-priced retail products you can market at fairs and local stores? Read how Darcy Teitjen has prospered with her potpourri business and how you can start one too. See the "Crafty Business" chapter on page 83.

10. Prop Rental—Find out how you can earn extra money by renting your antique furniture, collectible china, heirloom silver, and other items to photographers and food stylists. The beauty of the prop rental business is that you can continually rent out the same things over and over, making money each time! Read about Mimi Luebbermann's success in the chapter called "Odds and Ends," page 98.

These are the top ten businesses for moms at home; once you decide how much time you are willing to devote to a weekend (or spare-time) business, read through all of the 101 ideas outlined in this book. The perfect idea just might catch your eye and you will be on your way to the bank in no time.

INDEX